DIVORCE AFTER DEATH

A WIDOW'S MEMOIR

CONCHA ALBORG

Published 2014 by Shorehouse Books
Printed in the United States of America

ISBN 0-692-28441-9
EAN-13 978-069228441-4

Cover Design: Dwayne Booth
Photography: Bernard F. Stehle

"... the writing of a book, no matter how deeply, profoundly personal – if it is literature, if you have attended to the formidable task of illuminating the human heart in conflict with itself – will do the opposite of expose you. It will connect you. With others. With the world around you. With yourself."

Dani Shapiro, *Still Writing: the Perils and Pleasures of a Creative Life*

CONTENTS

Preface. Spoiler Alert

I decided to start writing creative non-fiction when my life became more fictitious than my novel. I wrote *American in Translation. A Novel in Three Novellas* (2010) while my husband, Peter Segal, was dying of cancer and I was taking care of him as his devoted wife. Immediately after his death and before I had a chance to publish it, I discovered that my supposedly loving husband had led another life full of extra-marital relationships. The man I thought was the love of my life did not exist. He had inspired Ewen, the likable character in my novel, who, in retrospect, was indeed fictitious. I still had time to change the ending, as my editor suggested, to match my new-found reality, but I chose not to. *American in Translation* is the novel I wanted to write when I wrote it and as such it was published, with the added bonus that it was even more of an invention than I realized. Since then I'm sticking with the truth and I write personal essays as my genre of choice.

As I think of the motivation for writing my memoir on widowhood, the personal essay seems like a natural transition in my career as a writer. My short stories have been labeled as autobiographical fiction since they are based on my own life but they have always had essay characteristics, such as personal comments about cultural differences between my native Spain and those of my adopted country, the United States. I have often played with a mixture of genres; both of my short stories collections, *Una noche en casa* (1995) and *Beyond Jet-Lag. Other Stories* (2000) are formed by linked stories that can be read as novels, since they share the same characters and plot lines, and my novel, *American in Translation* is composed of three separate novellas.

Thus, in this memoir I'm finally coming out, so to speak, as a merry widow forced by the circumstances in a post-mortem revenge of sorts. This is the only way I know of surviving the death and the betrayal of the man I loved. I actually don't like to consider myself a widow in the strict sense, since I hate the word itself as much as the concept. I only use it in census-like forms, otherwise I much prefer "single."

In some ways the betrayal freed me to seek a new partner in life as soon as possible. Later on, as I was writing this book, I realized that it forced me to fill the hole that Peter's death left. Now I know it was unrealistic to find someone to fill another person's shoes and meet all my needs: to fit into my home and life style, with children, grandchildren, career, travel. No matter how appealing I think my complicated life is, it was too much to ask of any man, certainly impossible for the men I met.

Widowhood has become a timely topic. We all know that women live longer than men and there are more of us baby-boomer widows each year. Joan Didion was one of the first to address the topic in her marvelous book, *The Year of Magical Thinking* (2005), followed in a few years by Joyce Carol Oates' *A Widow's Story. A Memoir* (2011). My intention is to write about similar subjects – sickness, death – with the added bonus of the betrayal and a good dosage of humor to make the widowhood medicine somewhat more palatable. More in the style of Nora Ephron in *Heartburn* (1983), although the betrayal itself is not what defines my life or this book. It's one of the markers, like being a woman, a feminist, a Spaniard, a mother, even a grandmother; themes which are all present in some part of this memoir. This book is not revenge, but I have to confess that it was liberating to see it come to life. Humor has saved me as much as the process of writing has healed me. The moment I wrote the letter in "Divorce after Death" and I saw myself on the page I started to relate to my situation as if I were a character in a book. I have my therapist, the late Josephina Miller, to thank for this. She suggested that I write the letter to Peter after his death to let him know how I felt. Never mind if he couldn't answer, that was his loss.

I should add that widowhood has also become a timely topic in Spain. During my last trip to Madrid for the yearly Book Fair, I met with Rosa Montero, who had just published her book *La ridícula idea de no volver a verte* (The ridiculous idea of not seeing you again, 2013). Her premise was to compare her feelings upon her husband's death with those of Marie Curie when she lost her illustrious husband and collaborator, Piere Curie. In fact, Rosa Montero hides her own feelings and probes much more into the life of the Nobel Prize winner instead of writing about her own loss.

That's not what I want to do, I don't want to hide. Some of the first chapters were written when Peter was still alive and as such they have stayed, without modifications. That's how our life together was, how his diagnosis felt, how his death struck me, how I loved him. For a time I thought to focus on my husband's illness itself, but I was repeatedly told that no one would publish a cancer book any more, since it has become an unpopular and an overworked topic. Thus, Peter's cancer is a point of departure present in the first part of this book, like "The End Game" or "East Meets West," where I describe my emotions during a hospital visit after my husband was diagnosed with terminal cancer. Despite the seriousness of the situation, life marches on, adjustments are made and, like others around me, a ray of hope is eventually found.

But the emphasis in this memoir is definitely on the changes the death of a spouse imposes. What does a woman, who has been married most of her life, do when her husband dies an untimely death? How does she reinvent herself and find her path through the maze of dating and career? Does she enjoy being alone or does she fear her new-found freedom? Never mind that dating has changed forever due to the internet and social media. Much to my daughters' chagrin, the stories about the boyfriends, like "The Merry Widow" or

"Eating Alone," where I share some of the dating trials and tribulations, are some of my favorites.

The pursuit of this illusive partner has taken me far. Thus, travel is a subject that I seem to relish. "Making Magic in Montalcino," where I make peace with the idea of traveling solo, is an epiphany of sorts. Let me warn you that, like in the first words of "Into the Woods," this is not a fairy tale, so don't expect a traditional happy ending.

Writing for me is not a solitary occupation. I am the least lonely, widowed or not, when I'm writing, and this book is no exception. I owe my sincere thanks to many people. Tamar Tulin continues to be a thoughtful and careful editor, who flags me every time my native Spanish gets in the way. Jack DeWitt, a true poet and friend with a fairy tale name, although he didn't make it into any of the chapters, read many of these and offered insightful comments. Paul Jablow, the one who got away, when he found a younger partner on another dating site, but stayed as a faithful writing pal and made several helpful suggestions as the savvy journalist that he is. Nick O'Connell, who hasn't read this book, but has inspired my writing through his insightful workshops in Tuscany and Provence. Dwayne Booth, my son-in-law, continues to be my favorite political cartoonist and he has, again, made the alluring cover for this book. And Philip Bertocci, not a prince or marriage material, but a true friend I can count on to venture with me into the woods from time to time.

East Meets West[1]

When I woke up, I had a headache. For a minute, I thought I was in a plane going to Spain on my usual yearly sojourn to visit relatives. In other words, a nightmare. I could see the gray clouds up above from where I sat next to a big window, and the images on the TV screen without the sound, although I usually don't watch movies when I travel. I could hear some announcements being made on the intercom as if we were getting closer to land or we had run into unexpected turbulence. I was even a bit dizzy and felt butterflies in my stomach flying up toward my throat. This plane seemed to be taking me to a place where I didn't want to go. Except that this time reality was worse than any bad dream or any trip to visit my family I ever had.

"Mom, Mom! Wake up, the receptionist is calling your name." Jane was shaking me urgently, trying to wake me up, a bit embarrassed. She had been waiting for us when we arrived at the hospital at six AM, although we had told her that she didn't need to come, that it wasn't necessary, that she could come later, after work. The surgery would take several hours.

I looked around the waiting room, conscious now of my new reality. Peter had been diagnosed with esophageal cancer less than a month before. It had been a whirlwind of activity: doctors' visits,

---

[1] An earlier version of this chapter appeared in *Letras Femeninas*, XXXI 1 (2005): 221-225.

second opinions, CT scans, MRI's, ultrasounds, endoscopies and biopsies—all this two weeks before the end of the academic semester. We had learned more anatomy and medical terms than we really wanted to learn: the pancreas, the gastrointestinal junction, an esophagectomy.

We could even say the euphemisms the doctors used as if they had always been part of our vocabulary: we were dealing with an aggressive tumor, the liver and the stomach could be compromised, the chemotherapy and radiation would follow protocol.

I couldn't see Steven, Peter's cousin, a psychologist who had helped us so much these past few weeks. He probably had stepped out to have a cigarette or make a call. I felt somewhat self-conscious around him and feared he was sharing our shortcomings with other family members. It was probably my paranoia showing. I knew this term from long before, having been the youngest and having been raised by overly critical parents.

"Dr. Kirkland is on the phone and wants to speak to you," the receptionist said with a suspiciously sweet voice, pointing to a door. I took the call in a small, dark room with a table and a few chairs; no windows there to fly away to Spain. Just the ideal place to receive bad news.

"Everything is going well, a little better perhaps than we had anticipated. We won't need to open his chest cavity. We'll make the second incision through his neck. That's less painful and makes for an easier recovery, since we don't have to break any ribs."

Uncharacteristically, I had lost my voice. "Is his pancreas compromised?" I managed to get out.

"No, it isn't, it's fine. I'll call you again when we are finished, in about three more hours."

"Thank you so much, thank you," I repeated, crying with happiness.

How relative life had become! I felt thankful then for the strangest things: that surgery was still possible, that it could have been worse, and that my husband had a chance. It wasn't supposed to be this way. Hadn't I married a younger man this second time around, a bachelor *bon-vivant* who made me laugh and could help take care of my two daughters? He sure had turned out to be a high-maintenance dude! Now thanks to him, I had earned a brand-new title without the proper credentials or experience: primary care-giver. Just what I needed, another title. This one was much harder than getting my own Ph.D. when the girls were still so young, more difficult than being an immigrant or a college professor, more intimidating than being the mother of two American teenagers. Now I could debut in my brand-new role of the wife of a cancer patient, thankful just to have Peter survive.

***

In the following few months, I sat again in the same waiting room, while my husband had several other procedures—another word with a new meaning—little adjustments here and there to keep him going. I got to know Carla, the receptionist, by name. I could do homework there or take a quick nap without fear of waking up in a foreign land. I could eat my breakfast in case of an early appointment or talk on the cell phone with Jane who was normally at work. The cousin psychologist had forgotten about us—not because we couldn't use one—but because we were becoming old hands at this. I didn't usually speak to anyone in the waiting room, hoping to get some reading done or finish all those *New Yorkers* which I didn't have time to read any more.

Most relatives sit together and confer in hushed tones as sad and nervous as I had been on my first visit. They run hesitantly when their names are called, as I did before. They cry quietly or laugh out loud, depending on the news. It's always the same routine, and yet, every time it's a little different.

The last time I sat in the waiting room, there was an Indian couple next to me. We said "hi," but didn't speak much more; I kept busy grading exams. The husband was talking in an animated voice in Hindi on his cell phone. I appreciated how difficult it was to explain the medical jargon to one's relatives. I heard him say "orthopedic surgeon" and "metal cap" in English. The wife, who was quite a bit younger than her husband, looked at one of those health magazines that can only be found in a doctor's office. She seemed more tired than worried. They were both dressed elegantly, much more than the average Americans in their casual attire. I, too, was dressed up in a classic suit, but not because of my "foreignness"—really. I had a students' initiation ceremony to attend at the university that afternoon. The couple probably interpreted it as good karma.

When Carla called me up to the front desk, I could see Peter's doctor waiting for me. I was surprised, since I didn't expect bad news. It was supposed to be a routine procedure.

"Dr. Kirkland, has something gone wrong?" I blurted out.

"No, no, everything is fine. I didn't mean to worry you. I just wanted to ask you a question." It turned out that the anesthesiologist, a Japanese intern, had recognized Peter's name.

"Is he a well-known classical guitarist? He thinks he heard him play some time ago. He even looked at his artist hands, but his nails weren't long enough." Dr. Kirkland seemed embarrassed that he didn't know his patient's occupation, as if it wasn't enough that he could save his life.

"No, he hasn't been able to play for months. The chemo has ruined his nails," I explained. Of course, knowing by now the anesthesia's effect on Peter, he probably counted to ten and promptly fell asleep before he could answer any questions. It was such an unexpected question, and here I was fearing some unforeseen problem, with my medical terminology at the ready. Anxiety is another old term in my repertoire.

When I went back to my chair, the Indian couple looked solicitously at me. They must have noticed my tension when I went to speak to the doctor. Perhaps they were encouraged by my elegant immigrant get-up, so similar to theirs. Now, they were telling me their life story. Their son, a student at Wharton, the Business School of the University of Pennsylvania, had suffered a skiing accident. He had fractured his knee in three places. They had arrived in Philadelphia the night before from Bombay; their flight was delayed due to the snow storm.

"That's right, I heard that the airport was closed for a while. You must be exhausted," I was trying to be sympathetic, but I really wanted to get back to my grading.

They had rented an apartment and the mother would stay until the son could get along on his own, however long it took. I was trying to follow their conversation, but I got distracted by their thick accent (I know, mine gets that way too when I'm jet-lagged) and my own worries.

I have no clue how we got from the skiing accident to Scandinavia. Next thing I knew, the husband, who turned out to be a scientist, was telling me about a study on opiates which had just been done.

"Although they don't grow opium in Scandinavia, it's too cold there," he said expressively. Now, that turned out to be an interesting topic. How I wished then I had paid closer attention. "The body releases opiates naturally under conditions of high stress and it relaxes us, allowing us to deal with difficult situations," the scientist continued.

He was trying to reassure me that I would be able to handle whatever came my way. He didn't know that I was a pro already at this, that if they gave diplomas for primary care-givers, it would be hanging in my office with all its cousins. Here, a complete stranger wanted me to think that everything would be all right, that our bodies can cope even if they betray us sometimes.

No wonder, I thought to myself, I've been drugged up all these months! I was so touched by their kindness that we ended up talking and laughing for a long time as if we were old friends.

I told them that since I am a film and literature professor, I hadn't heard of that study, but I use other images that help me keep going. Peter often said that I'm like a swan, that I look cool and beautiful on the surface, but underneath I'm pedaling fast as hell. Just to get even, I told him after his first surgery, that he looked like Ralph Fiennes in *The English Patient*.

"Yea, sure! That's because you wish you resembled Juliette Binoche," he answered without missing a beat.

And I felt better then, seeing that he hadn't lost his sense of humor. I explained to my new found friends that my husband reminded me of Platero, the little donkey in one of my favorite poetry books. He is vulnerable and delicate on the outside but strong and durable inside, as if made out of steel.

"That's right, that's right," the couple agreed in unison, "it's very important to have a positive attitude."

The closest image I could find was in relation to my new car. Although it is an automatic, it has numbers on the gear shift, a two and a three which I have no clue when to use. I guess they are in case of bad weather or emergencies of some sort.

"Well, I must be in fourth gear at least!" That made them laugh again.

Just when I felt I couldn't cope, I found myself driving fast, almost flying, under the influence of some unknown drug–some opiate I guess–all dressed up as the immigrant I thought I had left behind.

Rings Around Aunt Rebecca

Aunt Rebecca loved funerals because they were the perfect way to remind us that she was going to outlive everyone. She always took advantage of the opportunity and asked the attending rabbi to say a few prayers by the grave of her dear husband, Harry, who preceded her in death by almost twenty years. She particularly relished her sister-in-law's funeral, since they despised each other. Not surprisingly, considering that Aunt Rebecca had been carrying on an affair with Harry's brother right under the entire family's nose. I remember that day, when Aunt Rebecca stood in the front row and at one point almost fell into the burial well herself. My solicitous husband, her favorite nephew, saved the day by catching her in his arms and sitting her on one of the chairs where she should have stayed all along.

Her own funeral was a quiet family affair. Aunt Rebecca had lived so long that there wasn't anyone left from her generation to attend and, anyway, she had managed to alienate most of the younger relatives as well. She used to string us along with the promise of an inheritance. For a while, the chosen niece or nephew would indulge her every whim, taking her shopping, to lunch, to concerts, only to find out in short order that she really hadn't changed her will. The only heir was still Cousin Dottie, who hardly visited her, but was her only blood relative and a practicing Jew, not like me—related by marriage and a shiksa to boot.

She would have approved of her funeral, despite the small crowd. The same rabbi who officiated when Harry died was there chanting beautifully for her, too, and he even said a Kaddish for her dear departed husband. I read parts of a story I wrote about her. Granted, I didn't dare show it to her while she was alive; I was afraid she'd be angry with me. But it was very funny and it captured Aunt Rebecca's fighting spirit, her chutzpah and her moxie. We all had a good laugh with the part about my taking her shopping for cruise wear at Loehmann's when she was already ninety years old. After the brief ceremony, three cars carrying the few relatives followed each other to Hymie's in Lower Merion. Now, this part of her good-bye party she would have loved: tasty Jewish food (and not too expensive) in a crowded delicatessen (she was known to walk out when we were the only ones in a restaurant), very hot coffee (as she always drank it), lots of family gossip, and the best part—she didn't have to pay. I've never met anyone who loved a free meal as much as she did.

It surprised me that I cried when we finally got the call notifying us that Aunt Rebecca had died. I hadn't seen her in three days and I felt badly for not having stopped by the night before to say a quick hello, as I usually did on Thursdays after teaching at the university. I swear she died because her hair had been a mess lately and she knew I was planning a party for her 96th birthday. She would rather die than be caught with bad hair.

Soon after, we found out that my husband and I were the main heirs in her will. We had been the last couple sitting down in the long game of musical chairs we had all played for so many years. Cousin Dottie was so angry at us that she refused to pick up the sentimental mementos we put aside for her: a beautiful Seder plate, an antique menorah, a Kiddush cup. So much for family values!

"Listen, Dottie," said my husband, "be mad at Aunt Rebecca, who wrote the will, and not at us." But there was no reasoning with her. She walked away in a huff, and we never heard from her since.It turned out, that between the depressed stock market, her longevity and her expensive life style, there wasn't much of a fortune left after all. Aunt Rebecca had lived in a fancy assisted-living community in

Philadelphia since we moved her to Center City. She had agreed to the move to be close to us, her only condition being that we would take care of her to the end in the style to which she had been accustomed by her loving Harry. She had a luxury apartment on the 21st floor of a high-rise on Logan Square with a panoramic view of the Museum of Art and the city all the way to the Benjamin Franklin Bridge. Philadelphia has some beautiful neighborhoods, but it is one of those cities that is at its best from a distance; the higher and the farther the view, the less of a chance to see its imperfections.

"I always think about going to Atlantic City when I see that bridge," she told me once. Sure, with my father-in-law, I thought without daring to remind her, although she had admitted to me that they visited the casinos every chance they had.

Her move to the city cost me more than I bargained for, and I'm not talking about the impact it had on our inheritance. She decided to hire a service that would help her pack, tidy up her old place and unpack her things in the new residence. The problem was that in my role of dutiful niece-consort, I signed the paperwork without giving it a second thought. When Aunt Rebecca's moving expenses rose as high as her new abode, she refused to pay the bill, saying that it was more than double the original estimate. It was no use telling her that *Moving Solutions* had ended up doing more than double the work they were contracted for. Each time a worker had come in, Aunt Rebecca found another stack of old goodies she had forgotten she owned. Unfortunately, after the third bill and her third refusal, I, as the signer of the contract, received a court summons to settle the dispute.

I couldn't believe that I found myself in such a predicament. No matter how legal my status in this country, I always feel a tad uncomfortable in the presence of the law. It must be one of the curses of being an immigrant. As the date drew closer, I was a nervous wreck. It didn't help that I had to cancel my classes on the assigned day, something I never like to do. I was upset with my husband, too, who couldn't help me out of the situation—it was his aunt after all. So

I made him accompany me to the hearing although it meant that he was missing his work as well. When I tried to reason with Aunt Rebecca, she cackled something like:

"Don't worry, honey, we all know how smart you are. You'll win the case. An estimate is binding." Not as binding as having signed the darn contract, as I soon found out.

The minute the judge spoke to me, I knew I was in trouble. He began by calling me "Mrs. Segal" by Aunt Rebecca's and my husband's last name, which I was quick to correct. Just as quickly, I heard him make a sly comment about me being one of those feminists who keeps her own name. I felt like telling him that the woman from *Moving Solutions*—obviously a lesbian—was probably also a feminist, or that women don't change their names in my country. But I didn't want to spill the beans about being a foreigner; maybe he hadn't noticed my accent yet. It didn't matter; at that point I had already lost the case. I was asked to pay in full, plus court costs. Aunt Rebecca did end up making out a check for the total amount, but not without mumbling under her breath a number of times that maybe I wasn't as smart as she originally thought.

After Aunt Rebecca's death, for the sake of saving what by then had become our inheritance, we decided to clean out her apartment ourselves. We sure didn't want to give more money to *Moving Solutions*. Her front closet still had a few treasures such as several coats and a sewing machine, which looked as if it had never been used. I couldn't imagine Aunt Rebecca making her own clothes; maybe she used it for mending. The trench coat and her favorite winter coat, a long camel hair, a bargain we had found together in Loehmann's, were still in good shape. But there were also several car coats, which I had never seen her wear, stuffed in the back in plastic bags, smelling of moth balls. She had hats, gloves and other accessories neatly stored in plastic boxes. The only thing I kept is a short mink jacket. At first I thought it was too small for me. Aunt Rebecca was such a petite woman, but the styles are shorter now. I had it cleaned to get rid of the rancid camphor smell, and if I wear it with jeans and long, leather gloves, it looks trendy. At least her jacket is still going out to concerts.

There's nothing sadder than going through someone else's possessions. It's like undressing an old, sick person who doesn't want to be seen naked. It's a voyeuristic experience of sorts. Aunt Rebecca's life had been shrinking right in front of our eyes. Before I came into the picture, she lived in a large condominium near City Avenue in the Philadelphia suburbs. Later, when her Harry died, she changed to a spacious one-bedroom apartment with a small terrace overlooking the pool, an eat-in kitchen in addition to a large dining room, living room and a small den, which served as her office. I remember her sitting there, checking the financial page of *The Philadelphia Inquirer* with a magnifying glass and calling her broker with instructions, until my husband took over her finances.

Despite the lofty view, her high-rise in Center City was much smaller. Her kitchen was equipped as if she were going back to her entertaining days, but she didn't use it even once. The appliances still had the warranties inside when she died. She ate all her meals in the residence dining room and hid fruit and snacks in her purse in case she got hungry. In fact, she had stashed away all kinds of things she had taken wherever she went: paper napkins, paper towels—like those one finds in public restrooms—straws, servings of ketchup and mustard, sugar envelopes, even toothpicks although she had worn dentures for years.

The deeper we got into the bedroom, the sadder it became. She had cocktail clothes in abundance: sequin tops, party pumps, silk pants, but there were hardly any underwear left or nightgowns. Little by little, they got lost in the laundry or were left behind every time she visited the infirmary downstairs. It didn't matter how often I took her shopping, she would buy only one or two items at a time. If I miraculously succeeded in getting her to buy more or something expensive, she would return it with Cousin Dottie as soon as she could. Her bathroom was full of freebies from the cosmetic counters. I must confess to being an accomplice in this part of the scavenger hunt, since I used to save samples from *Clinique* for her. In fact, they were still there, waiting to be used on a special occasion along with the dressy clothes. She had hotel everything: shower caps, sewing kits, shampoo, but in all the years I had known her, she had never been away. I made a mental note for myself: when I'm ninety, I'm going to throw all that stuff away, or whoever cleans up my place will think I was cheap, cheap, cheap.

We decided to give Aunt Rebecca's furniture to a charity in the building itself, because they held flea markets and with the profits they organized events for the residents. Dear old Harry had been in the furniture business, so there were a few good pieces, but they just weren't to our taste. We were tempted by the four black lacquered chairs but decided against them. It was amazing how new the pink satin cushions still looked thanks to the cloth napkins that Aunt Rebecca kept on them (I realized then that the napkins were suspiciously the same khaki color as the ones in the downstairs dining room). Ditto with the sectional sofa, which was usually covered with a sheet, unless company came (not us, we were family).

One of the parting remarks from Cousin Dottie was: "I don't know why I'm bothering to tell you guys, but check out the Noguchi table, it may be worth something."

My husband saw one on the internet and it sure looked exactly like Aunt Rebecca's. We called *Modern*, a gallery in Old City, which specializes in that furniture style, but it turned out to be a knock-off. To think that we almost struck it rich with the faux Noguchi table! I ended up bringing home some glass pieces; one said "Lalique" on it, but I feared she had it engraved herself, and it was a fake, too. There were a few Limoges dishes with a faded gold trim, the last thing I needed, but I guess anyone can become label conscious.

The most intriguing things in the apartment were the family photographs. I could recognize Aunt Rebecca's features as a young woman. She didn't look as beautiful as she often claimed she had been, but she did have flair.

"What am I, chopped liver?" I used to ask her. I loved using expressions she had taught me.

Her hair was always blonde and meticulously coiffed. Her clothes fit her well and she often stared straight into the camera with a serious, self-assured look. The pictures with Harry were especially endearing. There he was—a tall, dark, Rumanian immigrant who towered over her and held her arm as if she would break. Little did he know that she would outlive him by so many years. Everyone used to say what a loving marriage they had, and I know how much Aunt Rebecca missed him. Just about every day, I would hear her say a hundred times: "My Harry this, my Harry that..."

They never had children. My mother-in-law assured me that they were a selfish couple and didn't want any, but that's not the story I heard from Aunt Rebecca. She shared with me that she became pregnant soon after their wedding, while they were still living with her parents in South Philadelphia. It was right before World War II, but when they found out that Harry was being called up, she decided to have an abortion and that ruined her for life. It was the only time I saw Aunt Rebecca crying. Her face was red, dripping with tears that messed up her make-up as I had never seen her. I mentioned this story to other relatives and no one had ever heard it, but I believe it. To this day, I'm certain she told me the truth. We were a good match for each other, because I missed my mother terribly. She had died in Spain before my thirtieth birthday and I really never stopped grieving for her. At the same time, Aunt Rebecca probably wished she'd had a daughter like me; maybe it didn't matter that I spoke with an accent or that I wasn't Jewish.

It was a sad moment when my husband and I finally closed the door to Aunt Rebecca's apartment. There, on the door frame, was the colorful mezuzah that we brought her as a souvenir from the Jewish Museum in Prague. We took it with us in her memory, although we knew that we didn't need any props by which to remember her.

In one of her last stays at the hospital, Aunt Rebecca surprised me by giving me the two rings she was wearing. One was a gaudy, gold cocktail ring that she loved, with a huge prawn-like setting. The stone in the middle was a pale coral with sapphires around it.

"Isn't this just gorgeous?" she told me in the condescending tone she could use; she always thought that I wasn't as stylish as she was.

The other was her diamond ring, a truly beautiful number with two rows of smaller diamonds and eight large Tiffany-cut stones forming a star in the middle. I was really touched, since I knew how hard it was for her to part with anything, and her rings were her dearest possessions. I didn't care what the jewelry was worth, but I knew it meant something. It must have been her way of letting me know that despite our differences, I was the closest thing to the daughter she never had.

For a long time I didn't do anything with the rings. I couldn't wear them because Aunt Rebecca's fingers were so much bigger than mine—amazing for the tiny woman that she was. Besides, they seemed much too fancy for my taste. But last summer, on a whim, I stopped on Jeweler's Row, where Aunt Rebecca had made a few stops in her day, to have them appraised. There were a mother and daughter doing the same thing in the small shop. It was impossible not to hear them: after the grandmother had died, they found out that she had been married before.

"There they were, a marriage license and this ring with tiny diamonds," the mother said.

"They are called 'no see ums'," said the jeweler. "It's worth $45.00. Give it to a relative."

"Didn't I tell you that we didn't even know that this marriage existed?" The mother sounded offended, but the daughter was the one really mortified:

"Oh, Mom, come on, show him Nana's ring. He doesn't really want to know all that."

"I hope your father was more generous," said the jeweler, who seemed to be enjoying the whole dialog.

"How much is this one worth?" asked the mother.

"To sell or consign?"

"Isn't it the same thing?" said the mother in an irritated tone.

"Not at all," the jeweler tried to explain.

"Mom, just keep it, for goodness sake."

Finally, the mother decided to have it cleaned and give it to her embarrassed daughter. That seemed to quiet her down, but now it was the jeweler's turn to become impatient. He was probably hoping that I was going to bring in more profits.

When it was my turn to get help, I felt defensive and started giving too much information as well: that she wasn't really my aunt, that it was my husband's relative, that I was a shiksa—all in trying to distance myself from the whole transaction. The jeweler took the diamond ring up to his eye and then went to fetch his thick magnifier, a chunk of glass the size of an ice cube.

"Now, this is another matter, to sell or consign?" he asked, still staring at the ring.

"I want to keep it, I just want to have it sized and appraised for our insurance policy," I said, feeling superior.

I was and I wasn't surprised when he told me its value. I always suspected that Harry may have been the kind of man who judges his own worth by the rings his wife wears. I was glad I had decided to keep it. I don't mean it to be a comment on my husband, but I was never going to get an expensive ring like that from him.

The cocktail ring was not something I would ever use, so I exchanged it for a similar one, in a smaller scale with an identical coral stone and diamonds around it, instead of sapphires. Actually, I wear it all the time for a kick, and it always brings a smile to my heart, thinking that Aunt Rebecca would have approved, saying what a smart shopper I was. The diamond ring still intimidates me. I take it out only when I want to impress someone, which isn't very often.

Old Men Look At Me

It isn't funny, of course, when men stop looking at women. After a lifetime of whistles, looks and a few fresh comments, which used to bother me since I consider myself a feminist, now the men I like don't look at me. It's more than that; they don't see me. I'm off their radar screen; I've become an invisible person. If that isn't depressing enough, I've noticed that old men not only look, but also stare me down.

I know; old men are men too. I should be writing this in Spanish, since political correctness is less strict in my native language. We can still say *la gorda, la rubia, la negra,* and nothing happens. While in the United States, there is hell to pay if one says "the fat one" (unless she is the one who sings last), or "the blonde," and heaven only knows what would happen if we were to say "the black one" and with good reason. I have an aunt who says that one of her granddaughters is *feíta,* which would be inconceivable to an American. Imagine a Gringa grandma saying: "One of my granddaughters is a bit ugly." Never!

So, let's agree that old men are men, but not the ones women want noticing them the most, never mind if we are feminist or not. Besides, since I'm closing up in age to the gawking geezers, I'm allowed to speak about them, and old women too, if I want to. I don't have to say "senior citizens." In other words, I've become an older woman myself; a woman of a certain age, even though I would be offended if I were to be called an "old lady."

If I go to New York City, I can tell immediately how men look at women intensely there. Maybe that's because it's full of foreigners who tend to be more aggressive. Men in the big city don't only look at women; they stare straight into their eyes, like a good bullfighter in Spain would look at the bull. In Philadelphia, founded by Quakers after all, men are not so forward. If they look, it's on the sly, unless you are in one of the blue-collar neighborhoods, and then it's every woman for herself. Even in The Big Apple, I've noticed that older men are the ones looking at me the most. But heaven help me, nowhere else is this more obvious than at the Jersey Shore.

Ocean City, New Jersey, for example, is fast becoming a retirement community, attracting all kinds of old people who come for the sun and the sea. Even though it's close to Philadelphia, a cosmopolitan city, as some would say, and Atlantic City, a bigger attraction, Ocean City has a personality all of its own. It's a long and narrow island, which serves as a barrier for the ocean, joined to the mainland by two bridges. The open side, facing the Atlantic, is full of wide beaches, with white sand that forms large dunes, giving the houses facing the sea some privacy as well as beautiful ocean views. The waves, though never like the ones in the Pacific, can be big enough for surfing during high tide or when a storm is brewing. On the bay side, there are no waves or beaches. Only the tides going in and out let on that it's also the sea. The bay is formed by canals shaped like fingers that hold the island in their grasp. These canals are full of summer homes with private docks, each at a different angle. There are only two or three public marinas for intrepid sailors coming from other shores or for locals of lesser means, like myself, who don't own boats.

For several years, my family had a place in the middle of the island, at its widest point. It didn't face the ocean nor had access to one of the bay channels, but we were in front of a wildlife refuge, where migratory birds stop on their way north or south, depending on the season. With a pair of good binoculars, we could see the ducks' nests and the tiny cranes after they had broken their shells and were wobbling around in the marshes.

I tried to go to Ocean City often, not only during the summers to enjoy the beach, but during the entire year, when there are fewer people around, to recharge my batteries. There I could write in peace or read to my heart's content, lying on one of the decks, even if I had to cover myself with a light quilt when the sea breezes were blowing. When I had academic work to finish, or if I had to grade or research a paper, it was easier if I could do it close to the ocean. I wasn't born on the Mediterranean for nothing (as Joan Manuel Serrat says in one of his songs).

Ocean City is not always as idyllic as it seems. Each year, there are more poor Hispanic immigrants working for a song on the island, doing all kinds of dirty tasks on the expensive homes: painting windows and shutters since the sun and the sea air are so hard on the wood, patching up the roofs that rot easily with the humidity, planting flowers, mowing the lawns, taking awnings up and down and moving furniture on and off the decks. I remember talking to a Mexican man from Oaxaca who was making an outside shower for the downstairs neighbors. At first he didn't even want to speak to me. Then he told me that he left his family behind in his country. He was sending them money until they had enough to join him in the States. I didn't ask, but I guessed that he was in the States illegally and that's one of the reasons he didn't want to speak to strangers. Also, it was probably the reason people were taking advantage of him and paying him low wages.

On another occasion, I noticed that in the big Super Fresh there was a Chinese food section (and I've never seen an Asian on the beach), a Jewish food section (the phonebook is full of names like Cohen, Segal, Ruben) and aisle after aisle of Italian foods (they must be the ones with the biggest appetites). But despite all the immigrant workers beautifying the rich folks' homes, there wasn't a decent Hispanic section. Not one to mince words, I asked for the manager and told him outright that there was some discrimination going on there. It wasn't that same summer, but now there is an entire area with Goya products, which happens to be a Hispanic company based in New Jersey itself.

***

Every morning during the summer months, before I started to write, I went down to the beach for some exercise. If it wasn't too windy, I would ride my bike on the boardwalk, all the way down to the lifeguard station. My problems could start right there. We all know that older people suffer from insomnia, and they wake before the sun comes up. So, even in the early hours, most of the benches that line the boardwalk are occupied by gaping old men. They would realize right away, despite failing eyesight, that I was no spring chicken, but that I didn't look bad for my age, either. At least I could still ride my bike, which most—if not all of them—stopped doing a while back. If one of them was almost completely bald, with those big dark glasses specially made for cataracts, I was vulnerable. And if I saw some other poor guy with a limp and a metal cane shining under the sun, I needed to watch out. The big fat ones, with Buddha-like figures, also would stare my way. The most dangerous were the well-preserved ones, who thought they were still debonair. I'm pretty sure that I saw one winking at me.

Did they think that I was their age? Did I look like I belonged to the same senior club? Was I not wearing riding shorts with a cute matching visor? I knew that I have some spider veins in my legs, but I was certain they could not see those from where they were sitting, between my speed and their eyesight. Yes, I dye my hair, but what did they know about that?

At night, Ocean City changes. The old folk must be at home watching TV or maybe they are in bed already. But the young crowd that was quietly sunbathing during the day, families with children of all ages, newlyweds who can't afford to go anywhere else on their honeymoons, all would converge on the boardwalk. Given my thirst for knowledge, I had to look up the word *boardwalk* in the dictionary. It's defined as "a promenade, especially of planks, along a beach or waterfront." Truly, a boardwalk is something unexplainable. It's part carnival, part arcade, part food court, part shopping mall. It's full of movie theaters, dollar stores and shop after shop of the most ridiculous souvenirs, T-shirts and general junk. And all this without a single bar or a club, because Ocean City was founded by Methodists, who were even stricter than the Philadelphia Quakers and forbade alcoholic drinks, and the laws have remained unchanged to this day.

My husband and I almost never went to the boardwalk, especially if Spanish relatives were visiting. It would be unimaginable. How could we explain that it's against the law to sell beer or to have a glass of wine with dinner? How to rationalize a beach without pubs or discos? I have to confess that on the few occasions I've been to the boardwalk with my daughters or American friends, I've enjoyed myself. Once Peter and I went, and we ended up in an arcade full of instant-photo machines, where, in a booth, we could fabricate a child to one's likeness. Since I already had two daughters from an earlier marriage, we decided to have a son. That's right, for ten bucks! First we had to answer a questionnaire as if we really were to adopt a baby. We had to decide his ethnicity:

"Should he be Hispanic or plain Gringo?" I asked only half jokingly.

"Well, he should be a mix, don't you think?" answered Peter without missing a beat, as usual.

"Fine. What about his hair color?" That being one of my pet issues.

One by one, we answered all the questions about eye color, size of the nose; even his age was specified.

"He should be at least twelve," said Peter. "That way we can leave him home alone." And we immediately agreed.

Then the "daddy" got in front of the camera, followed by the "mommy;" obviously a sexist machine. I have no idea what would happen if two people of the same gender wanted to have a child at the Jersey Shore. You waited five minutes and out came four passport-size pictures–just in case you want to travel with the kid, I guess. I was half-way emotional, as it well should have been with my first-born son. No sooner did we see our son, than we loved him already, although he was "*feíto*," a tad ugly like his dad. He turned out with a nose identical to his father's, too large, particularly for his age, with dreamy hazel eyes, from that side of the family, too. The bangs and his hair color were definitely mine; somewhat unruly and of an artificial mahogany shade. We named him Benjamin, given his last place in the family, and because it's a name that can be pronounced almost the same in English and Spanish.

The strangest part was that both of his "half-sisters" hated him from the start. The two of them said that he was very ugly, that his hair was like a girl's and that his skin looked green. I have to admit that he did have an olive complexion as do I. Our daughters made us promise, since they were familiar with our sense of humor, that we wouldn't frame Benjamin's picture and place it on the mantle, and that we wouldn't show him to anyone:

"Please, please, please, he's such a nerd!"

***

When Peter was first diagnosed with cancer, he loved coming to Ocean City. Here he could rest in peace (no pun intended) and, since it's so flat, he could still ride his bike without turning blue. But eventually, he wasn't strong enough even to climb the stairs to our second floor unit. Before he died, I decided to sell the place. I would have enough responsibilities keeping up the townhouse in

Philadelphia. It turned out that the downstairs neighbor, who had our key, had already shown our place to an acquaintance of his—a young widow with three small sons. I could only imagine what her situation was like in anticipation of my own widowhood. Never mind that I was pissed at my neighbor. I didn't know whether to call him a vulture or to thank him for his foresight. I felt better once I found out who the new owner would be.

As it is customary at the Jersey Shore, we sold the condo completely furnished, linens and all. I only brought home some personal knick-knacks and a set of Mikasa dishes with the shells for my name and the seagulls for Peter's (Concha means "shell" in Spanish and Peter's last name sounding like the bird). I had to give them away later because it just made me too sad to be reminded of our cozy summer place.

Before the closing, I went back alone to our home in Ocean City a few more times; those were emotional days. I was aware of how much I would miss that place, but it didn't compare with the bigger loss I would be suffering in a short time. I remember bargaining internally with myself. Perhaps if I sold the beach house, Peter would miraculously heal, and I could keep him for a while longer.

***

One of the things I loved best about Ocean City was going down to the beach an hour or so before sunset and strolling by myself at the water's edge. Often, at that time, the beach was virtually deserted. The children and their moms would have already left; the young crowd would probably be getting ready to descend on the boardwalk to hang out, and the old folk would probably be at home watching reruns on TV. There was enough light to enjoy the view. The pinkish clouds would join the deep blue ocean at the horizon. They had a unique color at that time of the evening: hues of purple, orange and pink with a touch of grey. Instead of old men, the birds would take over the beach. The seagulls were quieter and more pensive than during the day, and they stayed closer to the water. The sandpipers also would come down in the evenings, and the sparrows would fly low over the dunes. Sometimes, the moon had already made an appearance sitting low and coming out of the waves. If it was late enough, the first stars would be showing up, too.

On the very last day I was there, I was so distracted observing all this that I didn't notice a man approaching me. He was against the light, so I couldn't see him well, but he was tall and barefoot, like me, dressed in light colors with a sweater over his shoulder, in case the weather cooled. He didn't have a lot of hair, but it was carefully combed, rather stylishly.

"I'm sorry. I didn't mean to frighten you," he said gallantly.

"No, no. You didn't. I was just distracted," I answered.

"Do you come here often? I think I've seen you before."

And now he was closer to me, and I could see that his eyebrows and mustache were of a silvery shade.

"Yes and no," I tried to explain.

I told him that I lived a few blocks from the beach, next to the wildlife area, but that I didn't think we had ever met. He said that his house was on the bay side, on one of the channels, but he liked the open sea better at this time of night. He told me about his neighborhood.

"It's like an American Venice, don't you think?"

And I smiled because I knew that there is a summer festival called "Night in Venice," another unique spectacle of Ocean City.

We said goodnight right away; it was getting dark and I didn't like to get back home late. I didn't tell him that I was really saying goodnight and goodbye, that I would soon be all alone, ready to talk to tall strangers on a beach, no matter how obvious their pick-up lines.

Since that evening, I realized that old men not only look at me, but are now prone to start a conversation, if I give them a chance.

The Road Less Traveled
Reflections of a Spaniard on a Trip to Bolivia

The Richest City in the Country

Our group, nine members from Saint Joseph's University, arrived in Santa Cruz after a long flight from Philadelphia, tired but eager to start our immersion in Bolivian culture. We stayed at a Jesuit retreat center on the outskirts of the city. There was such a big contrast between the comfortable homes we had left in the States and the Spartan accommodations, yet since we had been warned, we were thankful to have a very small private room with a cot, warm blankets, a table and a chair. Down the hall were the bathrooms with running water and some fickle warm water in the showers. So what if the sinks were out in the hallway and the water only trickled from the faucets, we weren't supposed to drink the water anyway–not even to rinse our mouths. It would make it easier to use the water bottles. We never figured out when the showers would be warm. We could see some tanks on top of the roof and assumed that the sunshine served as the heater. The first ones to shower, preferably in the afternoon, should be the lucky ones, right? But it wasn't always that way–just another excitement in our day.

The grounds were quite beautiful, with some palms, grapefruit trees full of fruit and other trees we didn't recognize, almost a paradise to us. Despite the approaching winter, there were some plants in bloom and the grass was green. A cold front, which had settled in that part of the country, meant less mosquitoes. They call the chilly winds *surazos* because they come from the south, from the Patagonian pampas in Argentina. In the distance, we could see the mountains of the Cordillera Oriental and closer to us, the tops of some taller buildings. We liked sitting on the benches in the shade, waiting for the next activity or writing in our journals. For the time being, this was home to us weary travelers.

We did love the food, the soups in particular, and all the cooked vegetables and fruits. The desserts were tasty too, and soon we were used to the *coca* tea with each meal, highly recommended for the *soroche*, the altitude sickness, never mind that Santa Cruz is a mere four hundred meters above sea level. Thanks to the technologically savvy in the group, we were able to connect the small computer in the office to the web, and we felt fortunate to have a couple of minutes to send greetings to our families.

According to my guide book, Santa Cruz is the richest city in the country, although we had seen lots of poor areas on our way from the Viru-Viru Airport. In fact, the roads were in disrepair, clogged with trucks, SUVs and buses making their way in the endless traffic circles, with people hanging out of the doors going to work. I saw an interesting and controversial Bolivian film last year (the racy title alone, *Sexual Dependency*, gives you an idea of the content), which took place in Santa Cruz, and I recognized some of the places where the young gathered, like the McDonald's and the Burger King. In some ways, it could be any American city with plenty of places to have fun or get into trouble, only more chaotic and unpredictable. For example, unbeknownst to our hosts, there was some very disturbing graffiti outside the very walls of our residence: "En caso de violación, relájese y disfrute," in case of rape, relax and enjoy it. Paradise lost.

We visited several schools sponsored by Fe y Alegría, our host institution. In preparation for our trip we had learned that Fe y Alegría is "a movement for integral popular education and social development, whose activities are directed to the most impoverished and excluded sectors of the population." We knew from our reading materials that it was funded in Venezuela in 1955 and that at present it serves more than a million people a year in almost two thousand different centers. We were familiar with its philosophy of social and educational justice as well as liberation theology, or "the personalization of the new generations, deepening their consciousness of their own human dignity, promoting their free-self determination and their sense of community." The commitment made by the Jesuits through funding and human resources was also well known to us. But it was something else seeing these centers up close and personal. One of the first things we learned there is that a teacher makes less than $100.00 a month, not nearly enough to live on even in such a poor country as Bolivia.

One school had programs in the afternoons for children with Down's Syndrome and others with learning disabilities. We visited during parent-teacher conferences and most of the mothers (we saw very few fathers) brought their children and introduced them proudly to us. They had a kiln for their ceramics, sewing rooms, wood-working equipment and community gardens. The children had made arts and crafts projects as gifts for Mother's Day. The older students could even make furniture and sew their own clothes. The Santa Teresa nuns who showed us around told us that children like these would have been ostracized a few years ago. We laughed with them and remarked that even these children knew how to use the challenging Spanish subjunctive and could speak much more fluently than our bunch of *Gringos*! By the end of the afternoon, even the shyest ones wanted their pictures taken with us. They trusted us implicitly because their teachers told them that we were friends.

Magical Realism

One unforgettable place where we traveled was ten hours away from Santa Cruz in the southeastern corner of Bolivia, close to its frontier with Paraguay. Parque Nacional Kaa-Iya del Gran Chaco almost sounded like Lion-Country Safari or some of the entertainment centers where I took my own daughters when they were little. We did see all kinds of animals both familiar and exotic including cows, dogs, pigs, horses, *guanacos* (a kind of llama), *antas* (a hippo-like animal but smaller) and *chanchos salvajes* (a sort of wild boar). The problem was that the animals were all in the so-called road. In the 1930's, the Chaco was the sight of a war for the boundaries with Paraguay. Now, situated in a national park, this is where many of the Guaraní indigenous people live on 800.000 hectares of land given to them by the government to farm.

We left very early in the morning to make it on time to Charagua, where we were expected for lunch at another Fe y Alegría school. The road leaving Santa Cruz was paved and peaceful, but it soon became a dirt road and a deserted place. Innocently, I thought at first that the road was under construction–heaven knows that it needed some repairs. In fact, we did not see another paved road until three days later, on our way back. Fortunately, the van was very comfortable and there was plenty of room for us, our guide, Javier, the driver, Rocky, and his mysterious friend, Juan Carlos. I say this because we didn't know what his job was or why he coming on the trip. With a false sense of security, we hoped he was a mechanic, since our van seemed to have something wrong with one of the tires. We even bought a special tool from a stand on the side of the road to deal with this problem. Now, if people were selling tools, you know there was a chance we'd need them.

We were told repeatedly how lucky we were that it wasn't raining. It seems that the south winds are cold but don't bring rain. When it rained the roads were impassable.

"Well, it had rained a few days ago," said Javier when we reached a spot where the river had washed out the road.

Before we could respond, the van made its way across the current, something that happened a few more times during the trip. We did get used to the water crossing, and continued our chatter unperturbed or sang the songs that Guy, another Spanish teacher in the group, had printed in Spanish for us. Our plans to write in our journals or read were not realistic on this bumpy road. At one point, we could see a taxi stuck in the mud. Three men were pushing it, but it wasn't moving. Javier stopped and immediately the men in our group joined forces and pushed the car free. Old-fashioned chivalry is still thriving in Bolivia, and with this incident, we were immersed into the culture in one more way.

Just when we were feeling so proud of ourselves, we arrived at a construction area where a bridge was closed to traffic. We sat in silence as our guide rattled on in Spanish that there wasn't a problem, and we would use the railroad bridge. At times like this, there wasn't an advantage to understanding the language; I would rather not have known what we were up against. It helped that the train only ran three times a week, but it didn't help that the bridge was perched so high over the river Parapeií. Talk about altitude sickness! I can only compare this experience to getting into a carwash, but instead of putting the vehicle in neutral when our wheels were properly aligned, the driver floored the gas pedal. Lion-Country-Safari meets the white-knuckle roller coaster.

By the time we arrived to Charagua, Sister Carmen Julia, a nun from Spain, was nervously waiting for us. She had prepared a veritable feast of soup, salad, vegetarian lasagna and *creme caramel* for dessert. We were like children, giggling with the excitement of the eventful trip and also fearful since we knew it would only get more exciting. Buried in the park, Charagua is a cozy little town, the only one we'd see in three days. Sister Carmen Julia had some textiles for sale that were made by the indigenous people in the region. Each of them had a personal history that can be read in its design. The colors and dyes were bright and made from natural fruits and seeds. We bought some as gifts for our friends back home.

The end of May is close to the winter solstice in South America, so the days are short. It was getting dark, and we were a long way from Kopere, the first boarding school we were to visit. It was an *Arakuarendamí*, a place for learning, in the Guaraní language. Most of us fell asleep. When I woke up the van was surrounded by children, like bees around a beehive, screaming and smiling in the night. No dream we could ever imagine would have been more magical than seeing those young faces full of wonder and excitement staring at us through the windows. Once we were out of the van and Rocky had turned off the lights, we were in complete darkness, but somehow, the children could see us, and holding on to our hands they led us to the schoolyard. Javier rigged up a portable transformer and miraculous light surrounded us.

They had prepared an unbelievable *fiesta* for us. The children recited poems, sang songs, danced traditional indigenous dances while playing their own music. At one point, they put on animal masks, which they had constructed, and acted out the story of the *caporal de Potosí*, based on the harsh treatment of the slaves in the mines. Later, they would lead us by the hand and we joined them in a *cueca*, a big, frenetic circle of movement and laughter. We were smitten. The dinner of meat, *yuca* (a potato-like root) and rice was also served by the children. We took their pictures with our Polaroid camera; some of them had never seen a photo of themselves before and were in awe of their own faces. To them digital technology was not as special as instant gratification.

Some of the parents had made the trip to the school just to meet us. I spoke to Luis Alberto, who had traveled some thirty kilometers on horseback with his wife and baby. They had seven other children—six at this center. It is a big sacrifice to send the children to school. Not only do the parents miss their children terribly, but they do not have the extra hands at home to get the daily chores done. Without electricity or running water, they often go a long distance to find water. Additionally, they have to look wood for the cooking fire, grow all their food and make most of their clothes. But they are aware that if their children don't go to school, they will never know another way of life. Hermelinda, one of their daughters, is fifteen and she wants to be a doctor or a nun.

"Why not be both?" I asked her.

She told me that in Izozog girls who do not attend school marry at twelve. Then their parents are relieved to have one mouth less to feed. I was amazed at the level of socialization of these children. Each of them seemed to have "adopted" one of us and in broken Spanish (their first language is Guaraní) they communicated with us. Saying good-bye, though, was the same in any language: we all cried.

Soy Evangélica

The school where we stayed in Izozog was much larger and better equipped than Kopere. Some of us (much to the chagrin of the others) even had our own rooms and a private toilet which worked a couple of hours a day. No one had electricity after nine PM which we found out upon our arrival when we were given a candle and matches. Our visit was equally well-received here, although in a different way. For example, during breakfast the older students were butchering a large animal (was it a cow? I couldn't look) which would be our meals for the next two days.

Sister Benita, another transplanted Spaniard, showed us the school grounds. The children had well-constructed rooms, playgrounds and even a small library built with funds from Euskadi, the Basque government in Spain. One of their proudest accomplishments was the *chacro*, a community vegetable garden that the students maintained. They had planted all kinds of peppers, *yuca*, tomatoes, papaya, carrots, oranges, beets, sugar cane and corn. Given the semi-tropical nature of the land just about anything would grow. They had also designed an irrigation system. Marty, our food marketing expert, was avidly taking it all in, including some of the *ají* or chili peppers. The idea was that the students would go back to their communities and share their knowledge. We were surprised to find out that in this area of the country, Catholics were a small minority. Most of the families were Evangelical, and there were also some Mennonites like those we had seen on the road from Santa Cruz.

"But we all respect each other," Sister Benita assured us, "we don't have problems getting along."

We met the students' leaders and the town elders and we spoke with some women representatives. In all their activities, they showed a great deal of pride in their culture and traditions. We even learned a few words in Guaraní: *puama (buenos días), yasoropai (gracias)*. Their English vocabulary was better than ours in Guaraní. We wondered how long this isolated community could last. We heard that the World Bank already built a small airport not far from the school's land, and we feared that tourism could not be far behind (even if they'll have to build a better road before then). Linda, another participant, mentioned the implicit irony that in case of a nuclear war, the only survivors would be self-reliant, primitive groups like these.

The students had also planned a party for our last evening there that took place in the patio of the boys' dormitory. They had balloons, decorations, taped music, a few lights and a lot of style. Their costumes for some of the dances, which were familiar to us already, were sophisticated and elaborate and included frightening masks and matching outfits. Our dance in Kopere in the dark seemed even more innocent now. Amazingly, after the indigenous numbers were over, a "traditional" school dance broke out with *salsa* and *samba* sounds. In no time, the boys, in a reserved and formal manner, were inviting everyone to the dance floor. Cathy, the youngest member of our group, was in high demand. I noticed that Rocky (with his driving gloves off for a change) and his friend had joined us; they had cleaned up and smelled of after-shave. So that was the answer to the mystery: Juan Carlos had come for the party! Some of the girls would not dance. Sister Benita explained that the most observant Evangelicals are not allowed to dance, and the boys don't insist. I wished I had not been so self conscious about dancing, and had joined in the festivities. The student leader was making the rounds and when he came to ask me to dance, I quickly replied that I was Evangelical, hiding my awkwardness:

"Soy evangélica" and he moved on to a friendlier dance partner.

¡Ay Dios Mío¡

On our return to Santa Cruz, we were quieter and more reflective. It was hard to digest all we had seen. We felt tired from lack of sleep and hadn't had a shower in three days. Although we were ashamed to admit it, we missed the comforts of our simple residence, our home away from home. Perhaps because it was a Sunday, the road seemed busier and less menacing. A young woman, Debra, hitched a ride with us to Charagua. She was a doctor doing her year of service with the Guaraní people. She was proud of her work with them, but at the same time felt frustration with the lack of supplies and resources. On our way back, two little girls flagged our van to get to school. They looked to be six and eight years old, but they were actually older, ten and twelve—children here are small for their age. They had on *Little Mermaid* T-shirts, and I wondered if they even knew the story. In fact, they both seemed to have lost their voices and acted quite shy and quiet the entire ride, maybe because their Spanish was only rudimentary. We did see a smile on their faces when we offered them some candy and Oreos which they immediately twisted open to eat in two parts. Maybe they knew more than we thought.

We couldn't believe how far they had to go to get to school, and sometimes they'd walk all the way. There was an innocence in these children which was very endearing. A situation like this would be impossible to imagine in the United States. At the same time, they were very vulnerable. In one school, we had seen pictures of missing children and posters warning parents of kidnapping and illegal trade in human organs. Aside from all the children we visited in schools, we often saw students in uniforms going about in groups, but there weren't many children playing in the streets, as you often see in other Latin American countries. Being a child in Bolivia seems to be a serious proposition; they either start working at a very early age or, if they are lucky, go to school, no matter how difficult it is to get there.

And there we were, full-fledged adults, dreading the crossing of the railroad bridge. In some ways it was harder coming back, because we knew what was waiting for us. Two or three times we thought we were approaching the bridge only to see the long dirt road ahead of us again. Going over it initially had been unexpected and sudden, but not this time around. We teased Rocky and clapped at each hurdle: a strayed cow, an overflowing creek, a mud slide. We often used humor to get us through the difficult days. There were moments of hilarity that only our group would appreciate. One of the nicest parts of a trip like this was the bonding that took place. We really enjoyed each other's company and respected one another's weakness whether it was fear of snakes, wild dogs, mosquitoes, outhouses, or intestines in our soup.

I could never understand the Hispanic comic on TV's *Saturday Night Live* who screams *¡Ay Dios mío!* Why was it funny? I couldn't figure it out until we had to cross the bridge again. It became our password to the realm of the unpredictable aspects of this trip. When we arrived at the railroad bridge, there were families wearing their Sunday best strolling about. Some people were fishing from the highest part of the bridge. Small children teetered dangerously from it, and we were afraid to cross it? Again, with Juan Carlos' help (he had earned his keep after all), Rocky made his way onto the railroad tracks and we passed over the bridge while some kids waved farewell to us.

"*!Ay Dios mío, qué país¡ *" What an unbelievable country!

Lost in the Dump

In my trusty travel guide it says that Cochabamba, due to its mild weather, is the city of eternal spring, where the swallows never leave and the flowers are always in bloom. It's higher and drier than Santa Cruz by some two thousand feet, so bit by bit we were getting acclimated to the altitude (and drinking more *coca* tea). *La casa de la juventud,* the youth center where we stayed, was certainly idyllic with a gorgeous courtyard full of palms, a view of the Andes' peaks and a flowing fountain in the center. Our rooms were arranged in suites with private bathrooms (and warm water) and a central room for meetings, where a *refrigerio* (a tasty snack) was waiting for us when we arrived. The chapel, so peaceful and quiet, constructed in natural woods, seemed more like an Eastern place of meditation. But as we all know, every paradise has its glitch and the book also warns the intrepid traveler about the infamous dogs of Cochabamba. It seems that there are packs of wild animals that roam the city day and night looking for some tasty morsel.

Now I have to confess that I am the one who is afraid of dogs. My mother was bitten by one when she was pregnant with me, and I was born with this hang-up, probably from hearing about my mother's experience over and over. And sure enough, from our first night there I could hear loud barking and growling outside the walls of our residence. It sounded like the howling of wolves fighting amongst themselves. One morning, someone asked if we heard the shots at night. We guessed that some neighbors, tired of the noisy, mean dogs, had shot at them. So much for the placid swallows.

One afternoon, on the way to a technical school on the other end of town, we took a turn through what we thought was a short cut, but it turned out to be the city dump. At first we didn't even know that it was a dump, since so many roads are not paved in Bolivia. Then our van got stuck in a particularly bad spot and we quickly volunteered to push, since we knew from experience how it was done (We weren't a bunch of quick learners for nothing). But no, it wasn't necessary, there was simply too much weight in the van, so we just needed to get out and walk, and our driver would meet us on the other side. I guess we were a bunch of overfed Americans. As soon as we started walking, some skinny, big dogs appeared and moved in a determinate fashion toward us. John Jewel (and he is precious) was next to me, and I confessed immediately.

"You are afraid of dogs, really? I had no idea," he said.

The worst part was that the dogs sensed my fear and took some morbid pleasure in coming closer and closer to us and I swear they focused their eyes at my ankles. Luckily, the van made it up the hill just in time, and we climbed back into the comfort of the air-conditioning before being mauled alive.

I felt sad. Not only did I have to confess to a private foible, but the whole dump scene was depressing. The fact is the dump didn't much look like one. It resembled any of the many roads we had traveled: difficult to get through, unpaved, unkempt, uneven. The saddest part was that this was a dump with hardly any trash. All of it had been picked over, carted away, used for something else and probably eaten too. What little bit was left had been fought over by the hungry dogs. Little wonder then that they spent the nights barking away, howling in desperation.

Quechua Rock

Without a doubt, the most moving day of the trip for me was the one we spent in Tiraque, a small Aymará village, an hour away from Cochabamba. We left Lake Alalay and soon reached the *altiplano*, the highlands, where it was no longer spring. Strong, cold winds combined with the high altitude, made us aware that winter was approaching. Little Carlos and his wife, the caretakers of the residence, had packed us lunch. We joked saying that *los chanchitos van de excursion*, the little pigs go on a picnic (take it from me, it's funnier in Spanish). They were taking such good care of us, spoiling us really, and we knew they had planned some kind of a surprise for that evening, our last one there.

Our leader, Ann Marie, was very pleased when we arrived at the school, because the improvement was evident. Two years before, the boarding school didn't even exist and now there were several big new buildings and others under construction. It was so reassuring for us to hear that some kind of progress was indeed possible. Once again, a person from Spain–this time a young, lay woman, Isabel Pons–was the director of the school. Although she is a mathematician by training, she was explaining all about the greenhouses the students had built. Traditionally, due to the harsh climate in this region, the Aymará people have only grown corn, *quinoa* (a grain used to make flour) and a few other grains. Now they are learning through their children that they can use greenhouses to grow all kinds of leafy vegetables, which improve their diets and make them self-sufficient. The students had planted spinach, kale, different types of lettuce, carrots, radishes, potatoes. The purpose of the Fe y Alegría schools is to teach children, in addition to academic subjects, life skills that can be shared later with their communities, while preserving their traditions, culture and language.

Isabel is from Cataluña, a region in Spain very similar to Valencia, where I was born, and immediately we were speaking in Catalonian, our common regional language. She had been in Tiraque for two years and had one more left to serve. She missed her family terribly, although her parents came to visit last Christmas and a sister was about to come for a few weeks. I was deeply moved by the level of Isabel's commitment to the Bolivian people, and I wondered what it was like to live in such an isolated place, so far from her home. She confessed that she, too, often wondered what she was doing there. Many of her friends in Spain have gotten married and have started their own families. She felt that her life was on hold, but then she looked at the students, and it all made sense.

The Aymará children were beautiful. The girls were dressed in traditional short *polleras* (skirts) made from velvet, in dark, rich colors: aubergine, navy, burgundy, topped with a white lace or embroidered blouse and a warm sweater over it. They combed their long, shiny, black hair in two thick braids which they pulled to one side. Their faces, with a natural blush on their cheeks, gleamed in the sun. The boys kept their distance from the girls, not only in the dorms but also in the dining room and during their games in the schoolyard. As expected, their rooms were messier than the girls' rooms, although, interestingly enough, the boys were the ones washing the dishes (I could sense Isabel's direction here). At lunch time, together they sang a sweet blessing. Both boys and girls were shy in front of the camera at first, until they witnessed the magic of Polaroid, and then we couldn't take enough pictures of them: with their best friends, with their siblings, with a favorite teacher, with Isabel, with big Carlos, with our host, and with one of us *Gringos*... and they'd cover their faces laughing. It was endless; we took pictures until we ran out of film. Since I didn't have a Polaroid camera, I walked around taking other photos. Some students were playing soccer or basketball, oblivious to the picture-taking pandemonium. The older ones stood in circles speaking Aymaran amongst themselves. It's strange, but we never could tell how old they were. The younger ones seemed small for their age, but the older ones, the girls in particular, looked mature for their years, almost like short women already. However, despite the physical maturity, all were shy and seemed very naïve and vulnerable.

"Son buenos chicos" Isabel repeated proudly, telling us what good kids they all were.

Recess time was almost over and the previously camera-shy children were now in hysterics, still posing in different configurations. I was too sad to say good-bye, moved to tears and full of emotions that I haven't yet figured out completely. Was it A) Nostalgia for a more innocent time in my own country? (I do remember well the poor children in Franco's Spain). B) A desire to help these people like Isabel was doing? (Linda had mentioned that Isabel reminded her of me, a younger alter-ego). C) A sense of futility and frustration thinking that I couldn't make a difference? (How could I get away from my own responsibilities at home, where my own husband was battling cancer?) D) Pride in being a Spaniard like Isabel, or was it guilt somehow? Most likely it was E) All of the above.

That evening I was moved again during our reflection time. I was trying to explain my conflicting feelings to the group and what is like to be a Spaniard in Latin America. Suddenly we were interrupted by Big Carlos and Little Carlos who announced our almost forgotten surprise. They led us in the dark to an area of the courtyard which we hadn't seen before, a sort of multi-purpose room, *un salón de actos*, with a stage, where six young women started singing and playing Andean music. A long table with small candles, flowers, a variety of snacks (even some wine) and a chair for each of us were set up in front of the stage. Now it was Ann Marie's turn to cry, and the rest of us smiled with our mouths and eyes wide open. We knew they were planning a surprise, but we had no idea it would be such a professional event. The women wore white, tight pants with revealing red tops in different ethnic patterns; quite a contrast to the demure young girls in Tiraque. They played guitars, *charangos* (a small string instrument), *quenas* (flutes) and different types of indigenous instruments. They could sing in Quechua and Spanish, and they'd mixed traditional rhythms with rock beats. They were stunning! At one point I recognized the *cueca* that the children had performed for us in the schools and this time I didn't wait to be asked to dance. One by one, all of us, with our friends from Cochabamba, big, handsome Carlos included, held hands and joined the dancing around the room.

During the intermission, we found out that the group's name is *Naira* (which means eyes in Quechua) and they've been playing together for several years. One of the women was an attorney, two had established medical careers and the others were in other professions. The attorney's mother was their agent and she was busy selling us their latest CD. I have listened to it many times since we got back; it is quite trendy. Some of the cuts, like *Chuntunquí* and *Taquirarí*, are strictly traditional, while others–*Bosa, Son cubano, Instrumental*–border on rock. It represents a mixture of indigenous traditions and contemporary traits that can be found in many aspects of Bolivian culture; it is a new form of *sincretismo*, if you will.

Touching the Heavens / Tocando el cielo

La Paz is the most complex city we visited. In some ways it's a modern place, noisy and polluted, with tall buildings, frenetic traffic, a big airport. On the other hand, one can see many people–particularly the women–dressed in the ethnic manner (*polleras,* bowler hats, *ahuayos*, the carryall textiles across their backs), some beautiful *plazas* and official buildings all of which probably haven't changed much since colonial times. The international airport is up above La Paz, which is already over 3,500 meters in altitude (almost 12,000 feet, or four kilometers over sea level). This area, called El Alto, is a city in itself, with 700,000 inhabitants who have arrived from the countryside hoping to make it in the big city, but who had to settle in what is mostly an overcrowded slum. Suffice it to say that it's a city of contrasts.

On the road from the airport, we stopped to see the view which is breathtaking. This is true of many places in Bolivia; from a distance things can be beautiful, but the closer one gets, the more evident the problems are. Panoramic views are often spectacular; close-ups can be very painful, when one can see the poverty from front-row seats. As we stood there watching La Paz, gleaming in the early morning sunshine and clinging to a huge canyon with the snow peaks of Mount Illimani in the background, we were awestruck. Chris, the only African-American in our group, stood with his arms wide-open to have his picture taken with this impressive background.

"Finally, a black Christ figure" he said. How true. He remarked, that despite the overwhelming indigenous presence, all the Christ figures we had seen were white. In particular, he was referring to the Cristo de la Concordia in Cochabamba. It is made from white limestone and reminiscent of the one in Río de Janeiro, which also stood with its huge open arms, seemingly trying to protect the poor, the forlorn people of the Andes. Incidentally, there are several dark Madonnas in Bolivia like the beautiful Virgen de la Candelaria.

Having visited several schools in three major cities in the country, our main task in La Paz was to get acquainted with the central office of Fe y Alegría and to know its director, Father Enrique Oizumi, S. J. I have to confess that before this trip, I had reservations about its purpose. "Faith and Happiness" in Spanish sounds too much like the concept I had heard growing up in Spain, that the poor will get to heaven by having suffered and accepted–happily, no less–their fate here on this earth. To me, there was an implicit idea that religious beliefs were being used as an excuse to explain and accept their poverty. Not so; perhaps in name only (so fifties) is Fe y Alegría guilty of that sin. What we observed was a process of empowerment of the indigenous people, respect for their languages, cultures and traditions. They were given freedom of beliefs—remember the Evangelicals in the Guaraní territory—an acceptance of all people, no matter their faith or ethnicity. In other words, a very similar commitment to what the original Jesuits tried to do in their missions in Latin America in Colonial times, in contrast to their lay counterparts.

On the last evening of our trip, Father Enrique Ozumi invited us to his father's house for a good-bye dinner. As I write this now, I realize how fitting it was. In many ways, it was a culmination of everything we had learned in the physical and spiritual sense. His father, who had just passed away a few weeks before, lived in a truly spectacular penthouse. It had two floors overlooking the city, the top floor had two terraces, one open and the other glass-enclosed with a living floor underneath, also with panoramic views. If the view of La Paz is beautiful during the day, at night with a clear sky and its southern constellation, it is like seeing the reflection of the stars flickering on the side of the mountains. Each room was decorated in a different theme: there was a Colonial room full of antiques, a Japanese room with family pictures and porcelain collections that paid tribute to Father Enrique's heritage, a contemporary kitchen and the more formal dining room and parlor. The dinner was sumptuous: different kinds of melon served in the shape of a flower, kingfish for the main course, all prepared by an expert cook with Bolivian ingredients and Japanese aesthetics.

In some ways I was conflicted, because in the same day we had gone from the extreme poverty of El Alto, where we had visited a technical school, to the beauty and luxury of this penthouse. Here was where other members of the group helped to put my ideas into perspective. When I shared my feelings with our own Father George, he explained that for him it was that much more meaningful, because Father Enrique had been able to set aside this comfort and wealth to dedicate his life to the poor, to live in the community no matter how much he was giving up in the process.

I had made plans for my husband to join me in La Paz at the end of our trip. When Father Enrique heard that he was arriving the following day, he offered–insisted really– that we stay in his father's place, cook included. I turned down such a generous offer. It may seem silly now, but even for the few days I had left in Bolivia, I also wanted to be close to the people. Peter and I had a chance to visit some of the places that the group didn't see. On Sunday morning, we visited the La Paz's Museum of Art when we saw the announcement of a concert in the central patio. Imagine our surprise that the orchestra playing was from El Alto. This time it wasn't a program of indigenous music, but mostly Bach and Mozart. Having seen the living conditions in that part of town, the celestial music played by these young people and some of their teachers, all dressed in sophisticated black, was loaded with meaning to both of us. Just when we were so immersed in a third world situation and we thought we understood everything well, another surprise awaited us around the corner.

The Transplanted Spaniards. In the Moment.

Before the trip to Bolivia, some of my friends and family asked me why I would want to go to a third world country instead of visiting Spain again or some other glamorous destination. In fact, that was also one of the questions I was asked during the selection process for this trip. In part it has to do with taking responsibility for one's historical past. It isn't a simple *mea culpa*, but in some small way when I travel in Latin America, I want to witness and reflect on the contributions and the mistakes my country has made, because it makes me feel connected, assimilated into a historical continuum. In fact, of all the countries I have visited in Latin America, Bolivia has been one of the easiest, since in almost every school there was someone from Spain working for the indigenous people one way or another. I felt proud to share the same country of origin with them, but as a rule, it is not easy being a Spaniard in Latin America. I have a cousin who, when he encountered some hostility in his own travels, he'd answer defensively. It is not his ancestors who were responsible, he said, since he doesn't have any Latin American relatives; all his family lives in Spain. I don't share his smart-aleck explanation. I do believe, instead, that each of us has a chance to contribute; to be part of a new history (or is it only a story?) and make a difference in a unique way.

From my own experience, the Cubans, who are still suffering from the wrong-headed policies of the United States government, are also the most generous of hosts. They would never mistake policy with people. When they heard my unmistakable accent, they quickly told me about this or that relative who came from Spain and when they found that, in fact, I lived in the States, they'd run to give me some letter or small parcel to bring to yet another family member, immediately sharing what little they have. Connections, rather than disconnections, matter the most to them.

After leaving Bolivia, Peter and I traveled to Machu Picchu, in Perú, a place he had always wanted to visit and that had become even more pertinent, given his serious illness. My experience there was the exact opposite. Guide after guide pointed out the awful ways of the wayward Spaniards. Luckily, I wasn't wearing any significant silver or gold or I may have been asked to give it back. Perhaps it has to do with the cruelty of the Colonial Period in that particular country, but I had never been so conflicted being a Spaniard. So much so, that I started saying for the first time in my life–although this is true since I have been a U.S. citizen for many years–that I was an American; now that tells you something! On a few occasions they insisted—puzzled that my Spanish was excellent—that I could not be an American. To which I responded that I was a professor, which was also true and seemed to satisfy them.

The End Game

No matter how old a person is or how long someone has been terminally ill– one is never ready for the end game. My father passed away last year at the age of 96 and his passing brought back all kinds of memories about Peter's death that I had parked somewhere in the back lot of my memory. When Muriel, my father's wife for more than thirty years, called to say that my dad had died unexpectedly, I was in shock, despite his age and the fact that he was in the hospital with an appendectomy. I already had a ticket to Indiana for the following day, after the students' final exams, but he beat me to the final moment.

I believe that most people die as they live. My dad was convinced he was an orphan who no one loved and he died, as he lived, practically alone. Throughout his life, he made sure that he broke ties with as many friends as possible. Even in the family there were very few of us standing. Had he known how to bowl, he would have been a pro, all pins down. His legacy was discord, retaliation and revenge. My brother and my dad hadn't spoken to each other for more than twenty-five years. I doubt that either one of them remembered exactly what caused the final breakup—I sure don't. My brother had warned me not to call him when our father died because for him, he had disappeared so many years before. I thought he was kidding, but I later found out that he really meant it.

Eight months before his death, my father stopped speaking to me, too. He accused me of taking a ceramic vase my mother had made, which, in fact, he had given me many years before. I kept calling, but could only speak to his wife. I sent Christmas gifts and, although he kept them, he didn't acknowledge them. He had tried several times to banish me from his life, but I kept re-appearing. He sent enraged letters that I refused to open and I returned to sender. I think that, like my brother, I finally gave up. It hurt, but it didn't define me. It was easy to rationalize that our relationship, or lack of it, had more to do with him than with me. Nevertheless, when he died, I felt an irrevocable sense of loss.

He had gone to the hospital with appendicitis and had been writing to the very end. When I arrived at his house in Indiana, I found on the desk his last work dated April 17, 2010, three weeks before his death. The operation was successful, but he never made it out of the hospital. As can happen to people his age, a hospital-triggered dementia, caused by the anesthesia and painkillers, never lifted. He would attack the nurses and his wife, screaming that he was going to kill them all and that he would break their fingers if they came near him. He had to be sedated more and more to keep him from injuring himself. He didn't know where he was, he had never heard of Bloomington and he thought he was in Spain. He had switched completely to Spanish and kept clapping his hands and calling for the night watchman: "¡Serenooo! ¡Serenooo!"

When we lived in Madrid, the apartment buildings closed at 11 at night and the only way to get the doors open was to call the night watchman who carried all of the neighborhood keys with him even as he enjoyed a drink at the local pub. Years later, the *Sereno* was substituted by electric intercoms and people upstairs could buzz the visitors in. There are very few buildings left in Spain with a 24/7 doorman, only a few fancy places and the luxury hotels. The *Serenos* have disappeared the same way as the *Afilador* (the man who sharpened knives), the *Churrero* (the guy who sold breakfast donuts) and the *Trapero* (the man who picked up old clothes). And to think that my father was gone just as those vestiges of old Spain! It's so sad that he would end his days caught in a time warp; a place where he no longer belonged, in a time that no longer existed.

Muriel told me, that at one point in my father's madness, he thought he could see my brother and me in the hospital corridor, "But don't ask them to come in," he said to her, "because I'm not on speaking terms with them." Upon hearing this I didn't know whether to cry or laugh. So his mind was clear on that point, he wasn't so distraught as to not remember his feuds. I'm left with an overwhelming sadness that is also part of my dad's legacy.

I decided to stay in Indiana with Muriel for a few weeks and help her deal with the logistics after the death of her spouse, much as Lisa, my sister-in-law, had done with me after Peter's death. Disposing of his clothes was the easy part. We loaded Muriel's car and my rental car twice and took all the clothes to the Salvation Army. During the last few years of his life, my father only wore comfortable jeans in the cold weather and shorts in the summer, with warm shirts or just an undershirt (the wife-beater kind, ironically). His favorite shoes were some old Chinese slippers with holes in the toes. But the closets were full of beautifully tailored Spanish suits, fine leather shoes and fancy ties. I recognized the linen suit he wore for his wedding with Muriel and years later to my own daughter's wedding; it was still impeccable so many years later. I could detect his pipe and cigar smell in every article of clothing. Despite his emphysema, he never stopped smoking. Imagine how much longer he could have lived if he gave up that habit. The paperwork at the Social Security Office, the bank and the lawyers' office were just pro-forma, only a death certificate was needed. The calls to credit card companies and retirement accounts were resolved expediently.

Disposing of his porno collection, though, was another story. My father had taped hundreds of cassettes from TV shows. They were stacked on both sides of the chimney, under the coffee tables, on desks, in bookcases, in every corner of the family room. Neatly labeled, cassette upon cassette filled each closet of the three-floor house. I filled thirty-seven leaf bags (larger than trash bags) and put them at the curb to be picked up. Muriel helped me in silence. We all knew that my dad watched porn, but I, for one, didn't know the extent of his obsession. I remember that during one visit, when Jake, my grandson, was just a toddler, he disappeared downstairs with my dad and we all said: "Careful that he doesn't end up watching porno with his great-grandfather."

It is one thing to think that one's dad is a dirty old man, and another to see him as a sexual predator. I used to ask him about his affair with my aunt and other escapades I heard about from my family, which would infuriate him. Other times he would brag about his conquests, urging me to take notes for my next book: "But don't call me José Luis, as you did in your fiction; my name is Juan Luis." Here's to you, then, Dad. I realize that in some twisted way I confronted my dad about his sexual mores because I couldn't do that with Peter as I wish I could have. It was some kind of poetic justice doing it through a third party. I have heard that women end up marrying men who resemble their dads, but I never knew how much my husband and father were alike. Both were true artists, charming, hard working and intelligent, but both lived on the edge and died tortured by their demons, without true happiness and love for the people who loved them.

Muriel came to Philadelphia for Father's Day the year my dad died, and we had a small celebration of his life in my garden. My father had not wanted any public recognition and thus he was cremated in Indiana without any service, but we needed some kind of closure. I asked everyone to say something funny or poignant that they remembered about him. And that's how I wanted to remember him, too. I have enough good memories to last me a life time and enough bad ones not to miss him. I admired his energy, his work ethic, his thirst for knowledge and his wit. I have strong reservations about him as a father, a husband to my mother and even as a writer. Personally it was the end of an era. I can move from under his shadow now, I hope.

***

Peter looked like a wounded fighter that day when he came home to die with hospice care, three years after he was diagnosed with cancer. It was the middle of January and typically cold in Philadelphia. The hospital nurses wrapped his head in a white towel so he wouldn't be cold getting in and out of the ambulance. Only his spectral face, pure skin and bones, showed from under the covers. His eyes were open, as if in fright of what lay ahead. I'm not sure where his glasses were. I rode in the ambulance in silence, holding the covers, trying to find his hand, which was lost under the blankets. It was only four blocks down Pine Street from Pennsylvania Hospital, the same hospital where he was born 56 years earlier. The ambulance moved slowly, as if the driver was afraid the patient would break. The sirens were not on, the lights were not flashing, there was no hurry anymore. They parked at Fourth and Locust, right in front of the courtyard and they wheeled him out on the stretcher, through the garden and down to his studio, where the hospital bed had been delivered earlier that day. His sister Lisa was waiting for us. I must have looked as pale as Peter, since she immediately took over and helped move him to what would be his death bed. I had seen this operation many times before during Peter's illness. The patient gets lifted, sheets and all, to the bed. It's amazing how much a skeleton can weigh; I was never able to lift him without help, no matter how thin he had become.

Peter loved his studio, although he complained about it when we first moved into this house, because in Narberth—our suburban home—he had a separate carriage house, with its own entrance and its own address. There I could see him practice from the house, without hearing a note. I could see his students come down the driveway and disappear around the lilac trees. It smelled of him, that mixture of doggy odors and the Paco Rabanne aftershave that he always used. This studio in the city had the same old bookshelves full of his books and music, the same mission furniture, the same black and white striped sofa, with the old Persian rug from his bachelor days. The hospital bed had been placed facing the TV and the fireplace. Some of the furniture was pushed against the wall to make room.

The nurses arrived in a short time, but by then Lisa, who is a nurse herself, had already checked his port and his intravenous lines. I can't believe now that I learned so quickly to administer his morphine, clear his lines and check his vital signs. We had oxygen tanks at the ready, but never had to use them. Lisa was in charge of washing Peter and changing his bed pan. She tended to him at night, and I had the day shift. We made a good team, thanks to some unfortunate prior experience together; the two of us had survived the deaths of both of her parents in nursing homes. In part, that was the reason why Peter wanted to die peacefully at home.

Peter was never afraid of anything, or if he was, he never showed it. I remember his determination to get married, twenty-plus years earlier, despite the fact that I had one teenager and a preteen in tow and their father was as far away as he could be in California, without any visiting schedule. Peter used to tell me that I was a jewel, until he met my daughters and then he said that my house was a jewelry store. Much to the girls' embarrassment, he even had a sign made while he was away on some concert tour that says *"La Joyería."* It stills hangs in the basement of my house.

Peter was equally brave through his entire ordeal with cancer. Right upfront we were told that he had a 5% chance to survive five years, if he made it through the operation. Sometimes I wished we had played the Spanish game of not telling the patient and pretend he wasn't dying, like we did when my mother was sick. He endured the grueling operation that took more than six hours to complete, several rounds of chemotherapy and radiation, a central port in his chest for many months and an experimental study when there was no more hope with the traditional protocol. I don't know how we managed to laugh at many of the ordeals he had to go through. After the operation, for example, he carried a portable station with his intravenous nutrition and his medicines until he could swallow again. It used to make a hissing sound every few minutes, each time the liquids entered his body. We used to call it "The Gas Station." It was impossible for me to sleep in the same room with Peter and his station. He never complained, although once in a while I'd find him in the morning peacefully asleep with the entire system turned off.

In the hospital, Christmas Day was particularly trying. Usually I ate my meals in the room with Peter, just sandwiches or leftovers from home, especially at the beginning, when he slept most of the time. But I decided that this time I would eat the traditional holiday fare in the cafeteria, which I had checked out a few days before. I didn't want Peter to smell the turkey when he couldn't even swallow. The cafeteria was a bright, bustling place, with a huge picture window next to an attractive garden. It seemed to be full at any time of day. On Christmas day, I told myself that I was a big girl and could handle it. I would eat my holiday meal there and be thankful that my husband was still alive. The lines were unusually light, the food smelled delicious and looked homemade. There was sausage stuffing and natural cranberry sauce—my favorites. I served myself a big plate. When I entered the eating area, the shocking surprise turned out to be that I was the only person there. Two tables were set under one ceiling light, but the cafeteria was completely empty. The people in line must have taken their food up to the rooms or I don't know where. I ate my meal with tears in my eyes, sitting alone in that huge, somber place.

That same evening Peter said that he wanted to walk a bit down the hallway for the first time. I have learned that spending holidays in a hospital is not a good idea. Usually there is a skeleton crew, with only a few doctors making their rounds, since most of the patients have been released. Absolutely nothing happens in regard to treatment: no x-rays, no blood work, no nutritionists, no specialists; you are lucky if you get your sheets changed. On the oncology floor, there was a lounge-like room for families and friends, where one could watch TV or sit in a more normal atmosphere. Thank goodness that the room was empty, too, because Peter's feeding tube became disconnected and when he noticed it, he was covered from port to toe with sticky Ensure. It took a good while to get a nurse who could stop the yellow hemorrhage and clean the mess. That was the first time I saw Peter's surgical scars with huge metal staples, not something a squeamish wife should witness. No wonder he didn't want me in the room when the nurses came to take care of him!

Peter had learned his lesson and insisted on being released before the New Year's Day holiday. A few nights earlier one of his roommates had died of pancreatic cancer right there on the bed next to him and he was freaking out. Honestly, I wasn't in a hurry to have him home. I had grown accustomed to the hospital routine and having the nurses take care of everything, even if I had to kick butt once in a while, as Lisa used to say. I would arrive in the morning, still groggy from the sleeping pills, sit by his side, eat my breakfast, read the papers, work a little on the computer, talk to the nurses and the doctors about Peter's progress, go in and out to make phone calls (I was the only one still playing the Spanish game of not telling my relatives the whole truth). I would monitor the occasional visitors, although after more than two weeks in the hospital and due to the holidays, people were losing interest. The thought of having him home, responsible for all the possible complications, was daunting. But Peter prevailed, as he was known to do. I managed to summon an infectious disease specialist on New Year's Eve Day to drain his lungs of fluid. An x-ray confirmed that he would be able to breathe on his own, so an intern, who probably didn't want this cranky patient on his watch, released him late that afternoon.

My daughter Jane arrived in her SUV to help with his transfer; I could always count on her. Peter winced at every bump on Pine Street, but didn't say a word. I think he probably felt as scared as I did. It was too late to have the medicines he needed delivered. The intern assured us that Peter would be fine without them for one night. Despite the holiday, we were scheduled to have a visiting nurse first thing on New Year's Day. The thought of sleeping without being hooked up to the station was both liberating and frightening. I don't remember how I got Peter upstairs to our bed, but somehow I managed to get him into his pajamas and under the covers, without disturbing any of his medical sites. He fell promptly asleep, exhausted from his short trip home. Again, I ate some leftovers in the kitchen alone. One advantage of having a practically comatose husband is that I could read, write, watch TV in bed next to him and he didn't mind at all. Unlike the Fourth of July, when the trees are in full bloom, I could see the shining street lights through the bedroom window. I sat Peter in bed and snuggled next to him in time to watch the fireworks. I turned off the room lights and opened the curtains. "Isn't this romantic, Sweetheart?" I said. I was as happy as I had ever been in my life, with my husband in my arms, his eyes barely open, ready to start the New Year.

For the rest of his life, Peter remained on disability and never made it back to work. The management of his illness was like a full-time job. He took care of all the paperwork, his insurance, referral slips and made and kept all his appointments. I was able to teach, with a reduced schedule, through the entire time. I accompanied him to all his appointments, with the exception of two occasions when some close friends filled in for me. We attended seminars for esophageal cancer patients and their spouses at the Joan Karnell Cancer Center in Pennsylvania Hospital, met regularly with his nutritionist and by all accounts, dealt with our new life beautifully, not that we had any other choice. For a while I had my own therapist at the clinic, but soon I looked for someone else in the "real world." I found it hard to identify myself solely as the wife of a cancer patient. One of my complaints was that our sex life had completely ended, although I knew from the literature I read constantly that it didn't need to be that way. I couldn't imagine that all the cancer patients in the world—unfortunately, such a great number—were celibate. I now know that there were other reasons for Peter's distance, but at the time I felt guilty even raising this issue and didn't press it any further.

Up to a point, our lives went on and soon we had a routine guided by Jane's motto, "We can do that." In some ways, I felt more isolated than him, because I ran from the university to the house without wasting any time, while he had a string of visitors who would stop by on a regular basis. I wrote quite a bit those three years, because I spent lots of time at home keeping Peter company. He got well enough to meet me in Bolivia, where I had gone with a Saint Joseph's delegation, to make the pilgrimage together to Machu Picchu in Peru, a place he very much wanted to see. We traveled with his medical file: x-rays, doctor's reports, list of medicines, but never needed them, not even once. Due to the altitude sickness, people often used oxygen in the lobbies of the hotels, but Peter wasn't one of them. He had a way of rallying for special occasions, like the two interesting cruises we took, one to Alaska and another through the Baltic Sea. He also commissioned a piece of music by Jan Kriswicki and even got to bury his Aunt Rebecca, despite his fear that he would die sooner than her.

The night before his major operation, my other daughter, Diana, called from California, saying that they were expecting twins. Peter had a strange reaction to this news. On one hand he was pissed that he had to find out that night, as if the pregnancy was detracting from his place in the limelight. At the same time he was glad about the news, although he feared that he wouldn't live to meet the babies. But live he did and was completely smitten by them during the two years he knew them. Despite his obvious physical deterioration, I kept telling him to hang on, that he was young, that new treatments are discovered each year, that he was otherwise healthy, that he had a chance. He would have liked to go to Spain one last time, but I couldn't do that for him. A final tour to say goodbye to our friends and my family was more than I could bear. Some of the closest relatives made a pilgrimage and kept him company in Philadelphia for a few days at a time.

When Peter's cancer came back and all prescribed protocols had failed, he started an experimental study at the Cancer Center of the University of Pennsylvania. Those were the most difficult months. Peter's veins had collapsed and another port had to be installed in his chest just for the chemotherapy. He could swallow quite well, but his mouth was completely covered with cankers sores, so he had almost stopped eating, relying solely on smoothies and dietary supplements. There wasn't a trace of hair on any part of his body, eyelashes and eyebrows included. He had taken to wearing a wool cap, he was always cold and his voice was only a whisper of its old seagull cackle. I could tell that his original oncologist didn't think the experimental treatment would be useful for him. He kept telling us about the quality of life and maybe having fewer months, but being more comfortable. But Peter wouldn't give up. He made it through another holiday season and sat proudly in the *de rigueur* family pictures, looking but a shadow of his old self.

Peter started listening to operas early during his illness. He would lie on one of the living room sofas, put a DVD of the opera on the television screen and turn the stereo sound to full blast. By the time he stopped playing guitar, his music of choice was any opera he could get his hands on. He even went with an old friend to listen to the entire Wagner cycle *The Ring of the Nibelung* at the Met. It became an obsession. I walked around the house listening to my own music on the iPod, trying to keep my sanity. When I arrived home, I could hear his opera from the parking lot. It's hard to believe that our neighbors didn't complain.

The last days while Peter was still in the hospital, before coming home with Hospice Care, he was obsessively fidgeting with his computer and his cell phone. He seemed frustrated as if he couldn't figure them out anymore. Jane, the only one who could match him in technical ability, offered to help, but he wouldn't let anyone touch his equipment. I innocently thought that he was writing a meaningful note for me to hold onto after his death. From his hospital bed at home, he watched *Don Giovanni* by Mozart over and over, obsessively. He hadn't spoken in over a day, but he could hear and understand us. With his facial movements he would ask me to start the opera again. He finally died that night, ironically, listening to Donna Elvira's aria to Don Giovanni.

Diana had arrived from California the afternoon of his death and couldn't believe how the house had transformed itself. The entire downstairs looked like a death encampment. "Couldn't you see that

Peter was dying?" she asked. We could, but in theory only. Like him, we didn't know his death was imminent. "Why didn't you ask me to come over sooner?" Jane and I were repeating the proverbial "We can do this... and tomorrow." There was no tomorrow.

That very evening, with my two daughters and me at his side, Peter drew an imperceptive last breath. His sister Lisa had gone out on an errand. The three of us cried inconsolably for a long time. I thought that I wouldn't be able to shed another tear, but I continued to cry uncontrollably until his beautiful hands turned alabaster-like, with blue veins under the skin, cold first, practically frozen next. Lisa arrived, and she cleaned him one final time and wrapped him in a flannel sheet.

Lynn, a neighbor who is a doctor, came in to declare him dead, as we had planned. Some other thoughtful neighbors cleared the parking lot, so when Peter's other siblings arrived, there would be a place to park. His brother David asked if it would be all right to play the piano, and he played jazz until the ambulance came. Words didn't seem to be needed. Stephan, his other brother, didn't speak either. For a time, we were united in grief and music, something that had been a constant in Peter's life.

I remember getting on the phone and giving the people at John Hopkins University the final approval to come and pick Peter up. He had decided to give his body to science and be cremated later on. He had asked that there be no public service or any memorial, only the guitar piece that he had commissioned.

In Evening's Shadow by Jan Krzywicki (2007)
I.
Everyone stands alone at the heart of the earth
Pierced through by a ray of sunlight:
And suddenly it's evening.
II.
In a dark time, the eye begins to see:
The stand at the stretch in the face of death,
The far field, the windy cliffs of forever.
I meet my shadow in the deepening shade,
In a place leading nowhere.
A night flowing with birds, a ragged moon,
And the dead begin from their dark to sing in my sleep.
III.
I see you, love, I see you in a dream;
I hear a noise of bees, a trellis hum,
And that slow humming rises into song.
A breath is but a breath: I have the earth;
I shall undo all dying by my death.
IV.
Who but the loved knows love's a faring-forth?
Who's old enough to live? -- a thing of earth
Knowing how all things alter in the seed
Until they reach this final certitude.
This reach beyond this death, this act of love
In which all creatures share, and thereby live.
For soprano, guitar, violin, viola, violoncello
Poems by Theodore Roethke

I also remember the first time I heard myself referred as "the widow," "his widow," and how strange it felt. These few hours *post mortem* are the only ones in which I grieved for him officially. Forty-eight hours later, Jane would open Peter's computer to discover, before our incredulous eyes, that for many years he had led another life.

Divorce After Death

May 26, 2006

Dear Peter,

Today is your birthday, but instead of turning fifty-seven, it's four months since the day you died, although it seems so much longer. Despite asking you several times to make sure you left me a loving note I could read over and over when you were gone, you didn't write me. I've had several dreams about you, and in them I've already told you some of the things I want you to know. I've decided to write you. I hope you don't mind the repetition. It's such an irony that you didn't write the letter I could have read and I'm writing the letter that you can't read. I guess we are as distant in death as we were in life, although I didn't know it then.

Perhaps I should make clear that January 26 is the date of your official death, the one when your body left the house in the middle of the night to be cremated in Maryland, after the Center for Organ Donations finished with its job. You looked so white by then, drained of all color, transparent almost. I kept looking at your hands, which were still beautiful, perfectly manicured, as if you were going to give a concert that evening. It pained me to see your yellow teeth, your thin lips, your hairless brows and head with sunken cheeks, all too much like a skull. After your departure, Diana, Jane, Lisa and I sat in the living room and continued crying, as we had been doing for several hours. I can't remember the time we went to bed or how I slept that night. The next two days were a flurry of activity with people coming in and out, bringing flowers and food, the phone ringing constantly, although I hardly answered it. There were a million things to do, but I couldn't concentrate on any of them.

For me, your real death came two days later, on Saturday the 28th, the twenty-fourth anniversary of the day we met. After a quiet dinner, I decided to look for your promised letter. Didi had taken a flight back to California earlier that morning. Jake was playing hide-and-seek with Tía Lisa, Jane was doing the dishes, and it seemed like a good moment to hear from you. Your computer was on your desk where you had left it when we arrived home from the hospital. You had always been so secretive and obsessed with your damn computer. I swear you spent more time with it than you did with me, particularly in the last few years of your life. Even during the days before your death, when we already knew that you were coming home with hospice care, you were constantly fidgeting with it. Finishing my letter, I thought, since you always left everything for the last possible moment; leave it to you to be late for your own death. Jane came down to the studio to help me log in. She put to good use all the computer tricks you had taught her. Immediately she got a strange, horrified look on her face and tried to hide something from me.

The rest is part of my life history now and forever. There they were, several neat, labeled folders, each with the name of a woman: Jamie, Juanita, Josie, Dodi, Peggy... Hundreds of long, loving messages, some with pictures attached to them and many with references to trips, encounters, presents... Frantically, I read a few lines of each folder until there was no doubt of the kind of relationship you had with each of them. Michael left in silence with Jake. Jane, Lisa and I spent most of the night in utter disbelief; in shock, really. Your sister couldn't believe that her perfect brother had a double life. I was cold—in control—as I usually am in emergencies. I stopped crying and wouldn't shed a tear again for days, while, at the same time, I developed a sharp pain in my abdomen that extended to my chest and my back, preventing me from taking a deep breath for I don't know how long. I've never felt such awful pain in my life.

How could you? I kept asking myself over and over. You, who made such a point of telling people how much you loved me; you, who repeated incessantly the story of how we met; you, who were supposed to be such a gentle man, such a feminist. How could you? How could you ask me every night before going to bed, "who loves you most?" At the same time, many things started to make sense. Now, I understood why our cleaning woman quit suddenly—she probably caught you at home with your last girlfriend. Here I was taking care of you for over three years of cancer treatments and while I was at the university, you were entertaining at home. No wonder you insisted that I keep on teaching, that it would be "better for me." How could you? You schlamiel. Or is it schmuck? I, the shiksa, never mastered the proper vocabulary to describe someone like you. Never more appropriate the hateful Spanish word, which you despised, to describe what you did: *una judiada.*

Nothing compared to this profound sorrow: not my mother's death when I was still a young woman, not the three years of your cancer and not even your death. For weeks after this, your second death, I couldn't sleep for more than two or three hours at the time. I'd wake up startled, sitting up in bed with the realization, all over again, that the man who had been my husband for more than twenty years, the person I had loved most in my life, the stepfather to my daughters, the outwardly devoted husband, had been a fake. You were unfaithful for at least the last ten years. That's how far back the memory in your computers went, and up to the night before you died (we checked your cell phone messages as well).

It's amazing that someone who didn't believe in an afterlife has had such a busy life after his death. At first, there wasn't a day without a new find: a hidden present, a love note with big lipstick marks on it, a special recording with a personal message at the end. Jane—I don't know what I would have done without her—called each of your girlfriends and tried, as the grieving daughter, to get some information that could help us get some clarity, some explanation for your cruel, irresponsible behavior. They were shocked as well when she told them that there were several lovers, that they should be tested, that you had put us all in danger. I have something in common with each of them—we all thought we were the only one. Not that you'd care, but my own STD and HIV tests came back negative, although I need to be tested again in two months, to make sure, since you also had blood transfusions. I called two of the women myself, Josie and Jamie. I asked them both what they were thinking; they knew you were married – you often bragged about your family in your letters. "He swept me off my feet" was Josie's answer. You told her you were planning to leave me for her. I only wish you had, with the very first one... whoever she was. I would have saved myself the worry of taking care of you and your varied illnesses: chronic fatigue syndrome, clinical depression, two serious bike accidents, your drinking problem, the cancer and the unbearable pain of discovering your betrayal after your death.

I keep asking myself how I could not have known. How could I have been deceived for so long, when my own daughters used to call me "the detective"? You were certainly a master planner, an expert deceiver. It's a miracle that you didn't end up in jail, although you did get fired from your job, something else you hid from me. No wonder you didn't tell me or your doctors that you had reflux; you were so used to lying and covering things up that you hid your own medical symptoms. The cancer turned out to be a metaphor for your life, something corrupted that was eating you up inside—an insidious illness that finally killed you.

Sometimes I marvel at how close you were to being discovered. Josie said that she had a Christmas card ready, addressed to the two of us, but for some reason she didn't mail it. A note from Peggy, saying how much you had meant to her arrived on the day you died, but we didn't open it until a few days later. I wish I had found out in time to tell you to get out of my life, as your first wife did. Why, then, did you leave all this evidence behind? Did you mean to or did you think you had more time, that Death was just someone else you could fool? Why was I so trusting? I knew you had lied about your jobs, our finances, your past, but I never thought you could have been so deceitful and for so long.

I had an interesting visit with one of your psychiatrists, Dr. F.C.M. The other psychiatrist, Dr. D.S.C., said that he couldn't meet with us, although he did share some information with Jane over the phone. He knew of the affairs, but he thought you had been faithful since you became sick with cancer. You were lying to everyone, how could anyone help you then? This forensic psychology has helped us somewhat with the healing process. Having a term for your mental illness is a small consolation: personality disorder, narcissistic personality, bi-polar disorder, self-destructive wish, childhood full of trauma. I know it wasn't my fault, but I still wish I had known and if I hadn't killed you first, I would have tried to help you. I didn't deserve this, did I? Your loving wife, who took care of you over my own health concerns.

Don't worry, I'm doing fine now, although I lost 15 lbs in as many days and developed high blood pressure. My therapist said that I am the one in intensive care now. I worked with her and a bereavement counselor at the cancer clinic. I'm still taking an anti-depressant, and I will be for a while, but I've quit the Lunesta, and I'm sleeping well. I also took care of the surgery on my arm and it's healing. The pathology indicated that it was benign, in case you want to know. But it isn't easy. I keep asking myself: What went wrong? When? What happened to the happy marriage I thought we had? What part did I play in this travesty? Was it triggered by the demise of your musical career or did it manifest itself much earlier, as the psychiatrist suggested? Sometimes I don't know if I'm doing well or if I've been hurt so deeply that I just can't feel pain anymore. I've been trying to sort it all out. But in the meantime I thought I'd tell you what's been happening.

Basically, I'm divorcing you. Strange, I know, divorce after death. I'm moving fast, as I'm known to do, getting you out of my house and out of my life. Lisa took care of your clothes immediately.

After finding most of the documents, Jane restored all your old computers and we have given them to the Bolivia project. Jan Krzywicki helped me tremendously, packing all your music and guitar books. I donated them to the Temple Music Library. Such irony that you should have a memorial collection in your name, when in twenty years you never secured a tenured position there. I've saved the other music books to give to Yago, my nephew; I wonder if he suspected something when he lived with us. Your studio has become my library. I've been bringing my books from the university and rearranging them. I've never seen all my books together in one place before. I like them this way. Most of the photographs of the two of us are gone; I can't bear to see you holding me in your hypocritical embrace. I've replaced some of your mother's paintings with others more to my liking. The one of the blind guitarist, in particular, really gave me the creeps. Lisa was happy to take them off my hands. I sold two of your guitars, the Hauser and the Velázquez. I've shared the profits with my daughters and have started a college fund for my grandchildren. It's hard getting used to using the first person singular. Right now the girls don't claim you; Didi is very angry; Jane is just devastated, hurt beyond words. Fortunately, the little ones will not remember you. Michael and Dwayne, my sons-in-law, don't even bring up your name. I think they, as men, are ashamed of you; they are bewildered, really. You, who were so concerned about your legacy. Some legacy.

I've gone through all your files now. You were so compulsively neat about some things and such a slob about others. Forget the bi-polar theory, you were just a typical Gemini. It's sort of fun, you know, being able to bring up such things as your horoscope, without you complaining anymore. Yes, it hurts to keep on finding love letters and pictures everywhere, but sometimes it's funny, too, like when I started to read your letters to Juanita, copied straight from Nabakov. *Lolita* was always one of your favorite books, now I understand why. I started to laugh, and said I would have sent you right to the Dean's office for plagiarism. Some of the gifts I returned to the senders with a note asking them not to show up at your memorial concert, out of respect to our family. Most things have gone out in the trash. I've saved and copied just enough material in case someday I can turn this soap opera into good literature. It won't be easy, but oh, so tempting! Until then I'm thinking that I may share this letter with a few close friends. It's so painful to repeat the sordid story over and over. Your friends feel cheated and betrayed, too. One of the hardest tasks has been writing thank-you notes to all the casual acquaintances who wrote saying how wonderful you were. Don't worry, they may still think you are perfect, I got them all done and without a hint. You know me.

I met with Doug Johnson, your trusted pimp. Now, that day I was angry. He is the one person who knew the most and could have helped you and me the most. If only he had told me what was going on, especially when I confided in him that you were impotent and severely depressed. Instead, he called Josie when you were in the hospital, giving her the medical reports. I guess he was never my friend; over twenty years of marriage to his best buddy were not enough. He walked off in a huff when I asked him to stay away from your memorial concert. Like a lot of the things I planned for us to do together, the memorial concert was my idea. However, there won't be a memorial concert after all. I canceled it. I can only play the noble widow to a point – as my Jesuit friend, Dennis McNally, calls me. But now I know why you never recorded your own CD, despite all the equipment you bought. You were wasting your energy elsewhere. Forget your musical talent; you were better at making recordings of the personal kind.

I'm spending a few weeks at the shore now, not in Ocean City where we used to go, but in Brigantine, in the same development where the Dowdalls have their place. I've been making my own life, different from the one we had together. You would be proud of me. Just yesterday I figured out what was wrong with the lights in the bathroom (a fuse); loaded new music in the iPod; accessed the internet through AOL (for free); fixed my printer (no, it wasn't the ink cartridge—don't be mean); had my car towed when it broke down and rented another one, so I could get down here when I wanted.

Yes, all kinds of strange things have been happening at home, too. The basement flooded when the sewer backed up, the carpets had to be replaced and the staircase painted. I know how much you hated spending money on the house; "As if it wasn't expensive enough," you used to say. You won't mind now that I took advantage that the workers were already here and changed all the stairs to a pomegranate red; I've heard that it's a self-affirming color. While I was at it I had a new water heater installed before the old one broke down and messed up the clean basement (it was twelve years old already). The air conditioner is new too. It stopped working on the hottest weekend we've had so far. Remember that I used to say that all I wanted for Mother's Day was a repair person to follow me around for two weeks? How ironic that I should get my wish now. I guess I'm psychic after all, because I also have a good cleaning person instead of a husband, just like I said when I wanted to piss you off. It's also true that I gave up my husband for Lent, like a good, lapsed Catholic girl, as you used to call me.

My real Mother's Day treat was to fly to California to be with Didi, Dwayne and the twins. What a satisfying trip! I stayed at a hotel, but had lots of quality time with everyone. We even enjoyed lunch with my ex (you are, appropriately, my late) on the day that Didi received her Masters in Journalism from the University of Southern California. Your name hardly came up, as it would have normally, which makes me think that they already know about your secret life.

Some exciting news! I signed a contract with an agent, now that my fiction is more fictitious than ever, since your character came through as such a likeable fellow. In January I'll be going to Spain to teach one year in Madrid. I have arranged an exchange with Saint Louis University. The courses are all set and soon I'll start looking for my own place in my old neighborhood. And when I get back, I'm getting a new car. You guessed it, the Beamer I always wanted. I also went out on my first date, another musician. I better watch out, huh? He has retired and sold his instruments and now he's writing plays and movie scripts in New York City. It was my first blind date ever. We are always virgins in some curious ways. We saw a wonderful play, *The Landscape of the Body*, by John Guare. I couldn't remember when I had visited New York other than to hear an opera with you. I was thinking as I rode to the City that the last time I had a date was with you, I was thirty-seven years old. A lifetime ago. Too bad you are not here to give me some pointers.

I thought the holidays were going to be difficult, but by chance, we did spend Valentine's Day together, you and I. I stopped at the post office for a package that had arrived and it was your ashes. Such a small box for someone with such a big ego! We walked one last time through the neighborhood I love, arm in arm, so to speak. First, I left you in the luggage closet, but when it flooded I had to move you. Then I put you in the cabinet where you kept the presents from your lady friends; I figured you'd like that. Last month, Jane, Jake and I drove to the beach to scatter your ashes in the ocean, to wish you a *bon voyage*; you should have learned how to swim. It was sobering to see what a human life becomes: ashes and a few pieces of bone. At the last minute I accidentally fell at the water's edge and I got smudged with some of your dust. You didn't want to let go, I guess. I know you didn't believe in an eternal life, but may your ashes drown in as much sorrow as you've caused since your death. May you find yourself, forever, wherever you are, alone in the night, without the company of the people who loved you so much while you were alive. May your spirit find whatever little peace you deserve. That's your legacy.

I miss the man I loved. But the person I thought I married, the loving husband, did not exist. I don't know how or why, but I'm not angry at you, although for years you robbed me of my dignity, my intimacy, a sex life. You don't deserve my anger, I guess. But I am sad. I grieve the loss of my marriage, of my unconditional love and trust. I believe that, at least in part, you've paid for your deception with your life, with the awful suffering of your illness. If there is some kind of poetic justice (or is it revenge?), it's for me to embrace a new life, to live it to its fullest, to savor each feeling, knowing that you will not see the ocean again or hear the birds sing–the greedy gulls echoing your name–nor will you ever feel the breeze or smell the salt air. There will be no more birthdays for you. You will never play the guitar again or see my grandchildren grow. You won't taste another drop of coffee or wine. Almost every morning now when I wake up, I think to myself, if only for a moment; Peter is still dead, and I'm not ashamed to admit that I'm glad. This is my goodbye.

As ever,

Concha

Brigantine Beach
June 18, Father's Day, 2006

Cruise To Nowhere. A La Deriva

Last year at this time, Peter was still alive and we were on a cruise through the Baltic Sea. Despite all the traveling we did, we had never been on a cruise before that summer. I thought that cruising was *bourgeois* and that I would be bored to death sitting still on a ship; I'm known to travel as if I had roller skates on. But since Peter was too sick to follow me at any speed, we agreed not only on one cruise, but two. A counselor at the cancer clinic suggested it, saying that there would be medical facilities on board, that the food would be wonderful, that we wouldn't have to bother with suitcases, that there would be all kinds of activities if we felt like participating, that I could join excursions with other people, if Peter was having a bad day and wanted to rest and that it would be so romantic... I had a difficult time thinking, that what we knew would be our last trip together, would be romantic, but I gave in.

Looking for "cruise wear" turned out to be an interesting experience. I had seen this terminology before, but had never investigated that section of the department store. An entire floor ranged all the way from formal clothes, to matching his-and-hers blazers, from Bermudas in unbelievable shades, to garish print dresses and some rather sexy swimsuits, when what we really needed were comfortable shoes and some new underwear. Peter did buy a hounds' tooth linen jacket like one he had seen in *The Sopranos* and joked around every time he wore it, bragging about his mafia good taste.

The first cruise through the Alaskan Inside Passageway was not at all your typical fare, which is a good thing or we may have never taken the second one. It was a small ship, The Spirit of Endeavor, for about a hundred people, although it wasn't full. The itinerary emphasized the natural aspects of the landscape, an endless mountain range with snow-covered peaks that hugged the tranquil inlets. Despite the June date on the calendar, it was quite cold and rainy. The dress code was casual, and we all looked like we could have modeled for an L.L. Bean catalog. There was no entertainment on board other than the whales and the porpoises that would put on a show at unexpected interludes, sometimes with the cacophony of the sea lions in the background. The glaciers also obliged on several occasions, calving huge pieces of their azure ice right in front of our vessel. And the eagles, of course, hovered constantly between the coastline and the mountain tops. The cabin with two narrow cots was comfortable enough, but the room was not much larger than a camping tent. We all spent most of the day, binoculars at the ready, reading, chatting and playing cards in one of the multi-purpose rooms. The food was mostly native to Alaska—lots of salmon and Dungeness crab—prepared simply and served family-style.

One of the most amazing aspects of the trip, something I had never experienced before, was the luminosity. Given that it was near the summer solstice, there was light for more than twenty hours a day. The sun would still be shining when we went to bed, which wasn't very late, around ten PM, and it was waiting for us, no matter how early we awoke. Peter told me that it was even stranger in the winter, when it was dark for months on end. He made a couple of tours through Alaska in his concert days and was surprised to hear children playing in the streets at any time of night, like birds awakened in their nests.

During the trip, we were expected to socialize with each other, which wasn't so difficult since not only did we all wear the same uniform, but we shared many of the same values: yuppies who wanted to be different from the ones on the other, bigger cruises. Peter was the perennial elephant in the ship, the only one officially dying of cancer. His thin body and face with practically no hair gave him away, although no one dared ask about his condition and we didn't volunteer. The world-renowned musician had become the "ugly American," even if in looks only. Although we didn't have assigned dining seats, soon there were little groups that formed and we hung around together. We enjoyed talking with two British couples, whose accent contributed a lot to the civilized atmosphere, a couple of physicians from the Delaware Valley and a younger, funny couple from the corporate world. Sharon, Philip's wife, in particular, liked being the life of the party. She made me laugh with her story about the cruise to nowhere.

A cruise to nowhere was an event she attended in Florida with other corporate wives while the husbands were at a conference. I guess the glass ceiling was firmly in place in that company. It was an entire day at sea with all the amenities of a "real" cruise (not one like the one we were on): lots of food and booze. At the end of the day, the husbands boarded the ship for more wining and dining.

"The problem being that by then, Sharon was two sheets to the wind," her husband took over finishing the story. So much for the civilized atmosphere.

***

The Baltic cruise couldn't have been more different. The worst part is that I really loved it, and I don't care what it says about my social class. When we returned, Peter wanted to know what we'd have done if we could have gone on only one cruise. And I had to be honest:

"I would have taken the second one, you?" He preferred Alaska.

"True to our heritages," Peter concluded. He was the American while I was still a European.

In the official picture, taken by the crew, of us boarding the Westerdam, I have a big smile, despite the almost twenty-four hours of flights from Philadelphia to beautiful Copenhagen. Peter's face shows the exhaustion such a trip causes, especially for a cancer patient. He even looks shorter than me, which we usually hid well in pictures. His arm, though, is holding me tightly at the shoulder, as he always did in front of a camera.

Our "stateroom" deserved the uppity terminology. The twin beds had been made up together as a king, as we had requested. The dressing and bath area were almost as big as the one in our own home. Next to our private deck, there was a sitting area with all kinds of amenities: a mini-bar, a TV, a small sofa bed (for an unscheduled guest, perhaps?), fruit and champagne on the table. I have stayed in smaller hotel rooms and none as luxurious as this one. Waiting just for us, since they had our names on them, were two travel bags with more goodies and all kinds of information about excursions, entertainment on board, eating schedules and services. If we-weren't starving and jet-lagged, I would have spent hours just playing in the room with all the freebies.

I couldn't believe the amount and diversity of foods that were waiting for us in one of the many dining rooms, and this was only the holding tank where we were being served until the other thousand plus travelers arrived. To say that I was overwhelmed at first doesn't describe my feelings, but I became used to this luxury quickly and was soon complaining, like everyone else, when they ran out of shrimp or caviar or lobster at the seafood buffet. We had to dine at the assigned times – six o'clock for us, since Peter needed a long time to digest his food before retiring, much too early for the European in me. We also had an assigned, private table and waiters (I never got the exact count). Sometimes, I swear, Peter and I had more conversations with them than with each other, for there were so many decisions to be made: cocktails, appetizers, *entrées*, sauces, salad dressings, desserts, after-dinner drinks. We definitely should have taken a cruise before Peter had his cancer surgery. Holland American was making money on us.

Now I know why our dressing room was so large; we spent a considerable amount of time changing clothes. Several of the dinners required formal attire, and I mean formal. They were like proms for the real senior class: matching cummerbunds with the ladies' gowns, corsages—the works. The only difference, this time, was that the jewelry was real, too. Peter finally got some wear out of his white tuxedo jacket that he had purchased for a music festival in New England, where he played a concert years ago. His mafia jacket was perfect for casual nights. Finally, I attended the prom I never had in my Spanish high school. Of course, there was dancing on board. Turns out that Peter had been voted "Best Citizen" in his graduating class. I would have never guessed that I would be invited to the prom by someone as popular as he was. No wonder I look falsely radiant in those pictures!

It was easy to spend entire days on the ship. In the early mornings, I enjoyed reading on our deck, waiting for Peter to wake up, since he was sleeping so well. After breakfast I would exercise while he rested, either by power walking around the promenades, swimming, if it was warm enough and the canopy over the pool was open or doing Pilates in the gym. This was the one time in my life I was glad to have over packed since I was ready for every eventuality.

The evenings were full of distractions as well, even for people like us, who didn't want to gamble at the casino, play bingo or smoke at the bars. It's hard to believe that we were the same couple who had been content watching the midnight sun in Alaska. There was a different show to see every night, even if Peter turned his nose up at them. I guess he didn't remember that early in his musical career, he gave classical guitar concerts on the QE-2. Talk about playing for your dinner. Nevertheless, I don't think we missed one night: the magic show, the four-hand piano concert, the Broadway dancers, the comedian. I even had the tango dancers autograph their CD for me. That's another story: the opportunities for shopping on board were endless.

My favorite activities, though, were the excursions. I could pretend that I had my roller skates on and that I was traipsing through Europe as I had in my carefree days before meeting Peter. I loved Tallinn, a medieval town in Estonia. I parked Peter on a sunny bench in the main square and explored the quaint streets, taking pictures of its original architecture, a mixture of Russia and Europe with some of the best traits of both. Saint Petersburg alone was worth the trip. Peter had always accused me of being rather monarchic, and I guess it's true. I was enthralled by the magnificent palaces, Catherine's Summer Palace and, in particular, the Winter Palace that houses L'Hermitage, while, Peter, despite being an atheist, was seduced by the exuberance of the churches. We were both amused by the noisiness of the people and their pushy attitudes. They reminded me of my fellow Spaniards, those who need to make a living off tourism, but resent the tourists. We never knew when they were taking advantage of the ugly Americans, trying to sell us every possible *tchotchke*.

We saw Stockholm as if we were under water. A fine rain and fog enveloped the city all day, covering its majestic and solemn buildings in grey, making the red facades, the green roofs, and the gold cupolas stand out. I felt humbled inside City Hall, where the Nobel Prizes are given, thinking of all the intelligence that has stood in that room among the columns. Perhaps my favorite excursion was the architecture tour of Helsinki with a stop in Eero Saarinen's house. I could just imagine the commune-like life he established in that idyllic spot on the coast off Finland. We had to tender out of the ship to see the small town of Visby, a floating jewel, on an island off the coast of Sweden. It looked like an IKEA showroom come to life, covered by the roses of its country homes and surrounded by the ruins of its old walls, where the smell of the flowers and the sea breezes mixed as if by magic.

We didn't sign up for the trip to Berlin. I was there a few years ago, at a literary conference, and Peter wasn't feeling well that day. Besides, as a Jewish man, he hadn't made his peace with Germany yet. Instead, we treated ourselves to a Swedish massage. Our expectations of the trip and the promises of the travel agent had almost been fulfilled—at least as far as the food and the sightseeing went. But despite all the trimmings, our trip was not so romantic. I remember asking Peter:

"Do you think that the steward who puts the chocolates on our pillows and opens the bed every night, has noticed that we haven't messed up the sheets even once?"

I don't remember Peter's answer, because there probably wasn't any. I imagine that he shrugged his shoulders as he often did. He had bigger fish to fry; I know that. It was a sore point between us during much of his illness and even before. He didn't feel like making love to his wife. But I couldn't imagine that the unfortunately high number of people sick with cancer in the world had all given up their sex lives. I had read enough literature online about it to know that it just wasn't so, and it hurt. He never read a single pamphlet in the doctor's office as if he knew all there was to know about the subject.

I now reread my travel journal and it helps me understand in retrospect:

"I don't have any sexual desire for Peter either. I wonder if it has something to do with the anti-depressants I'm taking. It has to do in part, I'm sure of it, because I see him as he has become, and it's hard to feel sexual attraction. Besides he is not a romantic man anymore; he almost never touches me, unless we are in front of a camera. He walks behind me, resigned, with his hands in his pockets. He's so pleasant and charming, especially with other people around, but he is quiet and stoic with me. It's not that he's mean, but he's not expressive either. It's like he has used all his sensibilities on his music. I suppose that I'm getting ready for what is coming. It's easier to say goodbye this way. I'm going to be left alone; I'm going to miss him terribly, but this is no way to live, either."

At least, he agreed to the massage. The beautiful spa, done in marble, glass and chrome, was full of sunlight with a view of the

Baltic, drenched in sunshine that day. We each undressed in different areas and met in a room, which smelled of spices and citrus with new-age music playing in the background. A very attractive Russian masseuse was waiting for us. She explained that she would give us each a massage, teaching the other how to do it. I went first. The fragrant coconut oil she used felt warm on my skin and it became warmer as she spread it across my strong back. When it was his turn to try, Peter's hands had an unmistakable weight to them, even if I hadn't felt them for so long. I thought he'd be a fast learner, and he was. I became aroused and sad at the same time; both energized and relaxed. I thought I wouldn't be able to stand when the masseuse left us alone to trade places.

Living with a cancer patient is like having someone press the fast-forward button on the VCR. When you look again at the film, you recognize the actors, but a long time has passed, about twenty years (at least for me), and you don't know what happened. Practically in front of my eyes, my husband had been transformed into an old man. He looked and acted just like his father, who had died years ago at eighty-four. Peter's face, once broad and covered with a dark beard and a mustache, had become thin, with sunken eyes, devoid of any hair and completely pale. His lips, which were always thin, had almost disappeared, and his teeth, never his best feature, were yellow and out of proportion with the size of his new face. Despite the thinness, his neck was flabby and red, like a turkey's, with the tell-tale surgery scar of his esophagectomy running down to his chest. His abdomen, which used to be hard, had shrunken and a longer and much thicker scar marked it as well. His thighs, so heavy and strong when I met him – "soccer legs," he used to say – seemed much longer, as did his arms. Only his hands were still perfectly manicured, as if he were going to give a concert on board that night, beautiful enough to give a run for her money to the manicure lady down the hall. He lay on his stomach, with the towel covering his flat butt. I realized then that his back was like the beginning of the film: long and smooth, with perfect skin and broad shoulders, without any scars to remind me of any illness. Leave it to Peter to lie there, showing his best side to the Russian cutie.

***

This summer, I'm alone in a house at the shore in New Jersey. It's not the same one Peter and I used to own in Ocean City, which I had to sell before he died. It's quite a bit smaller, but it has a gorgeous, expansive view of the dunes and the sea. On sunny mornings, the blue band of ocean stretches all the way to the horizon, and Hopper-like sailing boats float effortlessly. With the binoculars I can see the dolphins playing. Later in the afternoon, the haze makes the water disappear and the green bayberries on the dunes take center stage. The birds: the marsh wrens, red-winged black birds, the swallows, are always chirping in different scales, like a well-rehearsed choir. In fact, I know when a storm is coming—not only by the color of the sky and the urgent wind—but by the way the seagulls and the piping plovers fly up from the beach, close to the decks.

It's really like an Impressionist's dream, where nature changes the landscape constantly. In the early evenings, when the tide has changed, I can hear the waves and feel the breezes coming through the windows from every direction. Later, the moon becomes a huge, golden mirror, surrounded by the black of the night. Then, even Atlantic City is beautiful, beaming in neon colors, looking like a huge cruise ship harbored in a foreign port. It may not be Copenhagen or Helsinki, but in the distance, it's still majestic.

Usually, I start to write early in the day at the dining room table, where I can smell the bowl of lemons and peaches starting to ripen. Surrounded by open windows, I can hear the birds and feel the salt air. It's like a widow's walk, those high windows on top decks by the shore to alert the wives that their husbands' ships are near. But I know that my husband will not be coming back. Oh, my God! I can't believe that I've used that word! I hate the "widow" word. I've spent my life using my maiden name, so I wouldn't be identified as a man's possession as in Mrs. and *Señora de*. I like it when people use my title, Dr. or Professor, without any reference to a spouse, and now I end up with a name that identifies me by the loss of a husband. It's equally foreboding in Spanish: *viuda*. The first time I had to check it on a Social Security application form, I almost broke down crying. Although I have to admit that I do feel some morbid pleasure when people call to sell something on the phone, asking for Mr. Segal. "He's deceased, take him off your list," I say curtly. It works better than any other line I've ever tried.

So much has changed since Peter died, especially after painfully discovering that he was far from the faithful, loving husband that he pretended to be, even during the long years of his illness. I wonder if it would have been harder to grieve his death than it is to grieve for our marriage. Maybe it's better this way; I can't really say that I miss him, knowing about his secret life. Right now I feel like I'm going through a divorce and that, hard as divorce can be, I've done it before and survived. Not that I have a choice, I wouldn't have written this script but, hopefully, I will have a chance to write about that, too, in time.

It occurs to me now that in some ways I'm the one on a cruise to nowhere, like Sharon, that woman in the Alaskan cruise was. Where am I heading? What is my life going to be like? My feet seem firmly planted on the ground, but I feel somewhat woozy, as if I were on board a ship, during a storm. There is an expression in Spanish that I've always loved: *a la deriva,* to be on the sea at the mercy of the winds. I try to translate it to English, but it doesn't do it justice: adrift. In some ways I'm still anchored, if not to our old beach house with the husband I loved, in some familiar territory, but I have friends nearby and my family comes to visit on weekends. It's hard to feel lonely with my little grandson around, waiting for me to take him to the beach to build castles in the sand. Last weekend, I even had a gathering here for some university friends, and we joked that Peter was still swimming with us in the ocean, since I scattered his ashes here earlier in the spring.

"No," I said. "He has drowned because he could never swim."

My friends are angrier about Peter's betrayal than I am now. Revenge can be sweet, even if it is only a small joke. Furthermore, I'm not drowning either. In the last few months, I have disposed of most of Peter's possessions: his clothes, his music, some of his guitars, his girlfriends' souvenirs and love letters. I have made plans to spend next year teaching in Madrid, which is something I couldn't have done before. I've taken care of some crises by myself: a flooded basement, a frozen air-conditioner, a broken down car. I have bought new pillows and linens for my bed, in case some of Peter's maladies are contagious. I've learned to choose wine (Albariño will do), and I get to play the music I want (how about some Billie Holiday?). In other words, I'm learning to cruise solo, even if it is in some uncharted territory.

Yesterday, I got off this ship and went to the Brigantine Beach Shopping Center, which is full of tanning salons, nail salons, hairdressers and beauty supply stores. What's going on here? Isn't this a beach town? How beautiful do the ladies need to be to take a swim in the ocean? Maybe this is evidence of a phenomenon known as the "Jersey girl," a high maintenance female species. Of course, the young saleswoman thought I was equally strange when I took advantage of being alone in the store and I asked her, sheepishly, if they carried vibrators.

"You mean a massager?" She asked me with an air of superiority, batting her long eyelashes. What did she know about massages, I should have asked her in turn.

I could have kicked myself for forgetting the vibrator with all the things I packed. What is a new widow to do? No wonder I feel like I'm on a cruise on the Baltic again, no sex. Usually, my evening entertainment has been one of the Almodóvar movies I brought with me, or I read a good book, now that the French Open has ended. Tonight I'll turn on some jazz, light a fragrant lavender candle and play with my new beach toy. Kidding aside, I have already learned that it feels less lonely to be alone than to be lonely when one is accompanied.

Today, I decide to take an excursion on my own to the Edwin B. Forsythe National Wildlife Refuge on the mainland, and I realize that I haven't been off the island in three weeks. I take a map, my binoculars, a good sun hat and plenty of bug repellent. I remember going there when my daughters were little and we got chewed up pretty badly. I found it without any problem, despite the confusing Jersey signs. The park is open from sunrise to sunset and there is no guard or entrance fee. Visitors pick up a self guiding wildlife brochure and take an eight-mile drive over the 40,000 acres of coastal habitat that is crucial for the preservation of migratory birds. It may not be the Alaskan coastline, but suddenly, I am in heaven. Even with the information in the brochure, I can't identify all the wildlife I see. I recognize white-tail deer in the woods; turtles, horseshoe crabs and ducklings hatching near the ponds and all kinds of birds, geese, ducks, cranes, and gulls flying over the marshes. I hear, but I can't see the finches or what I know is a woodpecker.

Since nothing is just what it seems, this park is not paradise either. True to their name, I don't see the native green flies, "no-see-'ums," but I can feel them biting me regardless of all the Avon Skin-So-Soft I put on. They are "yes-feel-'ums," alright. Just like my marriage, I start thinking again. Last week I finished reading Joan Didion's book, *A Year of Magical Thinking*, about the death of her husband, and I'm caught in what she calls the vortex effect. Nothing, or anything, can remind you of the past, and it catches hold of one's thoughts without escape. It's time to say what my daughters have taught me: "I'm not going there."

Instead of being tired when I get back, I feel like taking a walk on the beach. It's almost sunset, when the sandpipers like to walk at the water's edge and the noisy gulls are finally quiet, getting sleepy, standing on one leg. I remember how I had note cards made with a seagull and a conch shell representing Peter's last name and my first. I also found what I thought then were the most appropriate dishes for our shore house, a Mikasa set with shells and seagulls repeated endlessly on every piece. I'm so glad now that I left them behind in Ocean City. I feel the vortex effect coming again and I stop myself. I bend down to pick up a beautiful scallop shell. It isn't perfect, but it looks special to me because it has survived who knows how many storms in the open seas. I write my name on the sand with it, a C, an O, an N, another C, an H, and an A, Concha, a seashell. And I feel at peace, as if I were in my natural habitat. I may be on a cruise, but I'm going somewhere; I just don't know where yet. I startle the seagulls, waking them up, and they fly away silently, as I head back to the house before it gets dark.

The Merry Widow

My husband's Jewishness came out at Christmas time. The rest of the year one couldn't tell that he was a Jew. Well, technically he wouldn't be considered as one since his mother was Irish Catholic, although she converted to the Jewish faith after her marriage. In fact, Peter loved other Christian holidays such as Easter and always made a point of listening at least once every season to Handel's *Messiah*. He had been a singer in high school and loved most of the liturgical repertoire, which he knew by heart both words and music. But right after Thanksgiving, just in time for the Christmas sales, he started to complain about the holidays. They were too commercial, he didn't have time to shop with the end of the academic semester near, it was a waste of time and money and we didn't need anything. Never mind that I did all the shopping, wrapping and planning, even though it was the end of the semester for me too. He did write very clever notes with every gift, usually a riddle with hints to the content of the present, but decorating the house and getting a Christmas tree were unbearable chores. I started celebrating Hanukah our first year together, but that didn't help, it only added to his frustration with the holidays.

Usually we ended up getting a tree and Peter helped place the strings of lights, my least favorite part. But the decorating, the watering and, above all, taking the thing down, was left to my daughters and me. He claimed that I became downright aggressive when the Christmas tree started to shed its needles. I remember the year we had placed the tree in the sunroom, next to the picture window, and I suggested that we push it onto the deck through the window, instead of tracking the needles all over the house. Can I help it if he stood behind the tree, right outside the window, where I couldn't see him, and he almost fell to the garden below when I pushed the tree out the window? That incident had a happy ending though; from that year on we had an outside tree on the deck, decorated with straw ornaments, simple lights and food for the birds that provided the most natural decorations, albeit the occasional squirrel that threatened to topple the tree down. Of course, the plus side was that there were no needles inside the house and, supposedly, no aggressive wife.

I don't want to give the impression that Peter was a scrooge, he wasn't. He just didn't like Christmas shopping. Thus, he instituted the family tradition that we wouldn't get presents and instead we would do an event together. Later, when the grandchildren were born, only the little ones got presents. This was fine with me, because it seemed more in tune with the way I grew up in Spain. There, the Three Wise Men came on January 6th leaving toys for the children on the balconies or by the front doors of the apartments, where the children had placed straw for the camels and hard cider for the kings. Presents for adults became popular only with the Americanization of democratic Spain many years later.

Peter had the ability to create magic around him. It's not a coincidence that one of his favorite Christmas events was the trip to the Metropolitan for Mozart's *Magic Flute*. My daughters had never been to an opera and they got all dressed up to go to New York City. We had lunch in Café Fiorello before the matinee performance and walked down Fifth Avenue to see the lights at Rockefeller Center afterward. My favorite Christmas season event was the house tour the first year we lived in Society Hill in Philadelphia. He had hired a guide who took us at night to several historical spots, after a fresh snowfall. We visited the Powel House, where George Washington had danced in the second floor yellow room, the Physick House, where the first American soda was created, and ended up at The City Tavern, where we dined on authentic colonial fare served by authentically attired waitresses, although we didn't like the shepherd's pie.

The last Christmas before Peter passed away, we didn't have a tree. In fact, despite having such high ceilings and such big windows, we never had a tree in our beautiful Philadelphia house. I had given up on doing all the work, and we didn't have a deck where I could banish the tree, I guess. I remember that it was early January and Peter was bed-ridden with the effects of the last rounds of chemotherapy. I don't know what made me stop by IKEA, where there was a huge sale and all the Christmas decorations were drastically marked down. On an impulse, I bought boxes and boxes of ornaments: stars, pinecones, birds, beaded strings, icicles, balls in different sizes, all in bright red. It was a life affirming experience before I was familiar with the term. I knew full well that I would be alone the following Christmas and that I wanted a tree in my house and that tree would be decorated all in red with new ornaments. I didn't care if it reminded me of Macy's. Forget all the children's hand-made ornaments, all the traditional ones I had bought in Spain on different trips, all the kitsch musical ones to humor Peter, all the souvenirs from Christmas past. I was going to have a beautiful, huge Christmas tree decorated all in red to fit my new life as a merry widow.

* * *

Merry widow is the name I gave myself when I placed the personal ad in *The New York Review of Books*, but before doing that I had to experience Internet dating, an adventure not for the faint of heart. The first site I joined was through *The Philadelphia Magazine*, which seemed innocent enough for someone looking for some local talent. Little did I know that it merged with many other sites like "Marijuana Anonymous" and "Better Sex"—no wonder I was so popular. Can you imagine explaining this to my grandchildren: better sex with grandma! I had trouble with my profile from the word go; am I divorced, widowed or single? All of the above is not an option even though it fits me better than widow, a term I despise in English as much as in Spanish. For a feminist like me, who never wanted to change her last name to match her husband's, now I'm defined by his absence. Besides, I've heard that men don't like dating widows because they are still in love with their husbands and it's very difficult to compete with a dead man. Tell me about it. Degree is another stumbling block, since I'm told that a Ph.D. for a woman was as deadly as drug addiction. Actually, less so if you belong to "Marijuana Anonymous." Last book you read presents another stumbling block: *The Year of Magical Thinking* By Joan Didion. There I am, coming out of the closet as a widow again. *The Story of O* would be a safer bet for the "Better Sex" crowd. The photo is another important item. I had lots of casual snapshots, but only one portrait taken a few years back, definitely the only one that makes me vaguely resemble Sophia Loren. Of course I looked younger and it wasn't just because my hair was shorter, but I am sure that everyone's picture had been doctored, thanks to digital age technology. At least I'm not thirty pounds heavier. That's one thing about burying a husband, it takes your appetite away.

And what was I looking for in a mate? If I say "a financially secure man," it reads as if I were a material girl; if I say "an accomplished person," I fear to be classified as an overachiever; "professional" could be interpreted as snobbish; "sophisticated" as uppity; "energetic" as hyper; "youthful" as immature; and the list goes on. Soon I learned that "successful" means Republican, "in transition" means unemployed and "casual" means sloppy. Needless to say, I didn't strike it rich in this my first Internet try, and I'm not a material girl. I knew I was in trouble when an old geezer told me that instead of "Sophistication 13" for my handle I should have used "Arm Candy."

I realize that men may have horror stories about some of the women they meet online, but since I have only dated men, my experience is different. The "Journey Man" was one of the first (this took place before the TV series with that very same name). He claimed to be a CIA secret agent and was secretive to match. He told me that he was separated from his wife, but still lived in the same house, though on different floors. All this sounds so obviously suspicious now, although I believed it then. He was a traveler and did upgrade my ticket to Spain to business class (my first and only time in luxury) and came to see me in Madrid, where I was teaching that year. We also took a trip together from Naples to the Amalfi Coast and on to Sicily, but we didn't end up as friends. On the last day, while we were sailing on a ferry from Palermo to the Italian Mainland, I asked him for his share of the expenses and he covered his address with black marker before he gave me the check. At that moment I realized how little I really knew about him and felt very vulnerable. Leave it to a secret agent to make me disappear in the Tyrrhenian Sea!

When a widow starts dating, her friends feel free to make suggestions and offer advice. After all, we can be gullible and inexperienced in the ways of the world. I was told not to walk as fast as I'm used to or I would give a heart attack to some gentleman caller. Sure enough, Paul was stricken a mere two weeks after we met. Never mind that he was with another dolly on his sailboat in the Chesapeake Bay and I was firmly on land playing tennis with somebody else in Philadelphia. We had a good laugh about that when, in my best Little Red Riding Hood impersonation, I went to visit him during his convalescence, bringing him a basket full of fruit and sweets. We saw each other for a while, but I was suspicious of him because he always referred to women in negative terms. His daughter was nuts, his ex-wife was a wench and the Main Line ladies were spinsters. Heaven only knew what he called me when I wasn't around, the Speedy Spaniard? I started a tradition with Paul that has gotten me into some dating trouble. I suggested that I would like to fix him up with a friend of mine. Like his successors, he acted hurt at first, saying that it had to be me or no one else, but soon he called me back for more information. My girlfriend didn't like him either, she said he talked about himself all evening and had nothing positive to say about anyone. I saw him at a concert a few months later and he got even: he'd rather be playing banjo by himself than be out with my friend.

Some of my friends introduced me to their acquaintances, too. Linda so highly praised Joseph, an old flame of hers, that I imagined we were meant for each other and went to New York City to meet him full of expectations. We saw a terrific play, *Landscape of the Body* by John Guare, with all kinds of romantic connotations, but, unfortunately, Joseph spoke more to the guy sitting next to him than to me. He also made me pay for my dinner when I had taken the bus into the city and bought the play tickets myself. How do you tell your girlfriend that her buddy is a cheapskate? A word to the wise widows: be careful with introductions from friends, because not only you may not like the guy, but you may lose your old friends. Joseph was funny, though, I remember he told me that he lost his virginity once every ten years, I guess he wasn't up for renewal. He was also a runner and had the flattest stomach of any man in his sixties that I have ever met.

A very important consideration is what to wear on your first date. Just on principle I like to wear heels. It's sort of a revenge issue with Peter, who was just my height and didn't want me to appear taller than him. The problem is that men add inches on their profiles just as liberally as women take off pounds and I almost always end up being taller than the date, not an auspicious beginning. It's a balancing act to wear something sexy, but not trampy; something youthful, but not girlish; something stylish, but not intimidating. I usually wear jeans, as any respectable writer should, with a sexy top under a casual jacket that I can take off, depending on how the evening is going. Something form-fitting, yes; low-cut décolletage, no. I used to have this rule-of-thumb about clothes: would you wear it in Spain on your next trip? If the answer is no, then don't buy it. As a widow it morphed into: would you take this dude to Spain with you? If the answer is negative, then drop him. Of course that was the theory, now I have a mini-wardrobe that I keep strictly in the old US of A, such as my Pilates clothes, warm-ups and anything comfortable or over two years old. As for the guys, I have yet to introduce one to my family.

Dating in Spain is not any easier; I'd say that it's even more difficult. Women there seem to have given up when their husbands precede them in death. They go out with female friends and spend most of the time with family members. Somehow, they feel liberated and enjoy living without a male companion. Nevertheless, I wasn't about to give up during the year I taught in Madrid. I kept my eyes open and tried reconnecting with old childhood crushes, but they were all "happily" married or they were confirmed bachelors. I even called a well-known writer, a widower who gave a talk at the university and seemed very friendly. He said flatly that women were too distracting and he would never date again. He got up every day at 4 o'clock, wrote until 3 PM, spent the afternoon relaxing or with friends and was in bed by ten. That is to say that even though we were both in Madrid, we were nevertheless in two different time zones!

Having a potential boyfriend visit from out of town is a very risky proposition. I did it twice and lived to regret it. Luckily, Jim, who came for New Year's weekend, stayed in a near-by apartment that some friends had available, because the second I saw him at the airport I knew he had fibbed big time. Not only was he not good-looking, contrary to what he told me on the phone (he had a list of excuses for not sending a picture), but he was an oaf and three inches shorter than me, even without the heels. I have found out, though, that everyone can have redeeming qualities. Jim's Spanish was nearly perfect, and he could quote poetry in three languages. Lucky for him, he had already been to Spain many times before and wasn't interested at all in meeting my family. He was a fabulous cook and made several delicious meals for us: Codfish Callaloo and Smoked Salmon with Curried Potatoes were two that made it into my recipe notebook.

It was precisely while walking to the Reading Terminal Market with Jim to buy the ingredients for his recipes that I found out he had a second row of teeth. I saw him fidgeting with his tongue and at first I thought that he had a sexy piercing. But when I asked him, he explained that he had a small growth on his tongue because he, inadvertently, kept rubbing his tongue on his extra teeth. Why, you may ask, was I so interested in that? It's because I heard from a fellow writer that men love pierced tongues in women, it makes fellatio all that more exciting. I just wondered what effect it would have on the opposite sex, not that I was going to try it with him.

My other out-of-town visitor was even more disappointing. He drove from Iowa on his way to Key West in an old station wagon and, even though his hotel had a parking garage, he insisted on using my lot to save some money. The only problem was that the next morning his car had been broken into, all the contents had been rummaged through and his computer and other gadgets had been stolen. I felt terrible for him. We spent the day reporting the theft to police, talking to insurance companies, and trying to find a glass replacement place open on Sunday. How's that for a first date? By the time he left, he was very angry at me and a series of nasty e-mails followed. He claimed that I should have warned him about my dangerous neighborhood (it isn't), and I told him that it's stupid (it is) to leave a vehicle, with out-of-town license plates, full of stuff, in plain view.

So, from that day on, I have limited my escapades to the local variety. Now I know that in the first few minutes of meeting someone, you can tell if you are interested in pursuing a relationship with that person or not. I don't believe in love at first sight, but there must be chemistry, something I was never good at in school. No wonder the advice for new widows is to meet with potential suitors only for coffee or lunch first, not for something like a dinner and show, to say nothing of overnight visitors for a holiday weekend. In fact, I'm curious about an American dating concept, speed dating. According to its definition in Wikipedia it started in late 1998 in Beverly Hills (of course). It's something like a round-robin event since "most people quickly decide if they are romantically compatible and first impressions are often permanent."

Let's face it, you get what you pay for, another American concept, so for a reasonable fee I joined eHarmony which promised to be a better site for women like me, whatever that meant. Right away, I thought that any man who completed the long personality profile had to be a serious candidate. In addition to the usual tripping points, there were some that should have been simple, like race; I had the choice of White, Latino or Hispanic, African American, Asian or Other. What if you are white and Latina like me, do you check Other? I'm proud of my Hispanic origin, so I choose that category, but it implies that I was some other color than white. It turned out that I was getting playful with all the questionnaires and I ended up describing myself in a clever way as a truly international woman, liking Italian food, Chilean wines, Spanish cinema, German cars, American men and French love.

The rules on eHarmony are very strict. First, you have to wait until the matches according to your parameters are sent to you, then you can wink or send a smile (only one per match), a set of questions is sent, then a list of "must haves" and "can't stands," followed by e-mail correspondence guided by eHarmony standards. Only if you have survived all this protocol, do you start corresponding outside the network or speaking to your match. If you are lucky, you have his last name by then and you can start Googling him, the only way to get true information. What really happens when you are being bombarded with so many "perfect" matches is that you immediately start looking for imperfections and the smallest detail makes you click "close that match." If an innocent says that *Pretty Girl* is his favorite film, immediately I deduce that he is sexist or a player; close that match. If he makes a spelling mistake, back to the drawing board; close that match. Since you know who is watching you and when was the last time they were on the site, if he doesn't answer immediately; close that match. Likewise, the silliest details can attract you to the ideal man: a clever remark, his knowledge of Spanish, a perfectly trim beard, a cute dog… and they say that true love is hard to find.

I conclude that I like imaginary men best. I love the virtual profiles but as soon as the real person shows up… oops, he has huge ears! I started to make up a composite man, sort of a Mr. Potato Man, remember him? I like Edward's face, Paul's answers, Bert's age, Steve's degrees, Howard's proximity, and the last book that Philip read. Wait a minute, how did Dallas, Texas get through the radar, didn't I set 120 miles or 200 kilometers parameters? It must be one of the so called "Flex Matches," when one of the preferences doesn't match but it's otherwise a good match. Now I know better and I don't even open those; close that match, *finito*, kaput, *basta*.

Someone who makes it through was Boy Toy, a 46 year old stand-up comedian. Never mind that he is closer to my oldest daughter's age than to mine, lucky for me the term "cougar" didn't exist yet. He travels a lot and works every weekend. Does this sound familiar? He is finishing a Master's in Communications. Do I tell him that I put two daughters through graduate school and two husbands through two Masters and one Doctorate in Musical Arts? He gives good phone and makes me laugh when I ask him about his profile, since it says that he is looking for a woman 38-72. He should change the 38 part, he says without missing a beat. We meet for dinner in Old City and I find out that he is vegetarian, no problem. He is bald, no problem either (they all are), through his open shirt I can see that he has lots of gray hair on his chest, which I like. He doesn't limp, doesn't have a fat stomach and he walks as fast as I do. But we rush through dinner because he has to run to play basketball with his buddies, definitely a problem; I should have closed that match.

The phone conversations before meeting are very insightful. If he gives long answers, he's in therapy. Suits and scientists give short answers. I usually ask them what is in his bedroom; if he says stuff, he's messy. If he says a big TV, a sound system, his computer, it's easy to deduce that he's a nerd. Now, if he starts describing the linens on his bed, then we are talking, unless he is into Mommy Porn. Because there is already so much information on a dating site, it's amazing how personal a phone conversation can be. I found out on our first talk that one guy used a pump to have intercourse due to his prostate cancer surgery. Since online has become synonymous with out there, getting to third base should be easy, right? Not.

As a writer, I always struggle when I have to write the sexy parts. I even attended a workshop at a University of Pennsylvania Writers' Conference on writing the sex scenes. It's not any easier dating in widowhood. The sex talk comes first and let me tell you that one shouldn't do what I did when a shy man, another writer in fact, asked me what my proclivities were. He practically ran out the door when I said I liked orgasm. Say "intimacy" or "tenderness," corny as it may sound, and don't blurt out that you never go to bed with Republicans, or it may come back to haunt you. I usually break the ice with a bit of humor, letting them know that I have Googled them and asking if it was as good for him as it was for me. I felt better once I realized that men are as concerned about their physical appearance as we women are. Turns out that they like candle light, soft music and a flimsy nightie as much as we do, anything to create a sense of allure to camouflage our aging expectations.

I've paid big time for writing "Old Men Look at Me." I didn't know then that I would be looking at the senior geezers myself in a short time. I should have grabbed one when I still could. Later, cancer made even Peter appear thirty years older than his fifty-some years. It was as if someone had pressed the fast-forward button on the VCR machine and, needless to say, it's impossible to rewind the darn thing. In addition to telling me that I walk too fast and that I make them trip, the men I date often complain about a pulled muscle, when they have a limp, of a blocked tear duct, when their nose runs and of insomnia, when they fall asleep at the movies. Of course, I don't say a word about my allergies and I hide the surgical scar on my arm along with several other maladies. The fact is that I'm becoming rather fond of older gentlemen; I have this illusion that the older they look, the younger I appear!

Sometimes I ask myself what Peter's profile would say if he had filled one out. It would be something like this: divorced man, no children, self-assured, charming, musician, teacher, fluent in Spanish, loves travel, good food and beautiful women. Last book read: *Django Reinhardt. The Life and Music of a Gypsy Legend* by Michael Dregni. Favorite film, anything by Pedro Almodóvar. His picture would show his long hair, a rascally smile and a trimmed beard. In his bedroom he would have a wall-to-wall bed. And, obviously, I would have answered his ad. My therapist tells me that I can't be comparing anyone to Peter and I know that with my head, but my heart wonders.

When I met lusty Bernard, he said we would make love in every room of the house just to get even. He kept his word. A photographer and a poet he's also one of the cleverest men I have ever met. He wrote a haiku for every occasion: "Blank face at every turn, no angle in any corner" for writer's block. He used to leave little notes quoting phrases he claimed I said: "I'm an aspiring virgin with a fallen angel" or "I just want quickie sex and long days and I'm getting the opposite." He used to tell me "I'm in love without you" or that I loved him just the way he wasn't. I would tell him that he was a great editor, the problem was that he was editing my love life. Just because I make up my bed when I get up in the morning and I like my home picked up, he thought that I run a tight ship and the only person that could make me happy was a West Point graduate or someone like that. Maybe it was true that I was disagreeable when he disagreed with me, while he was quite charming when I disagreed with him, as he claimed.

One evening, while we were watching the Academy Awards in my living room, Bernard was lustier than usual, which is already saying a lot. He was pestering me to make love right there and then, on the leather sofa, with the TV blasting and the lights on. I was trying very hard to keep him at bay, paying attention to every Oscar category and checking the awards on my cheat sheet as they were given. Suddenly, he appeared in his birthday suit, with only his knee socks on, proclaiming:

"And the winner is…*The Full Monty.*"

Bernard is proof that breaking up is hard to do. There was never a good time to do it and my foreignness played a trick on me when I chose the last day of February, on a leap year, without knowing that it was also Sadie Hawkins Day. How was I to know that, according to the American tradition, on that precise day, a woman can ask a man to marry her? I had invited Bernard to dinner at a cozy Mexican restaurant and he accepted thinking that I would promptly ask for his hand. He almost cried when I proceeded to give him my prepared spiel: that we were too different, that we wanted different things, that he was a great guy, but... that I wasn't over Peter's death... that we could be good friends. I didn't know whether to laugh or cry when he started telling the people on the next table what I had just told him, that I wanted to break up with him on Sadie Hawkins Day, no less! Half of the restaurant got involved in the discussion, so much for an intimate atmosphere. Bernard's parting words weren't so funny; according to him and for my information, I don't need any more good friends, what I do need is a good lover! But Bernard was not done yet. Later on, he decided to answer my own ad under a fictitious name, "Pangelingua." We had several hilarious e-mails until I discovered his identity through the familiar syntax and his quirky sense of humor. Luckily, my linguistic ability came in handy before I made a fool out of myself and agreed to meet him again.

Yes, after answering a few personal ads in *The New York Review of* Books without success, I decided to write my own, after all, I wasn't a writer for nothing. I was intimidated at first by the secret code nomenclature: GWM for gay, white male, WJF for white, Jewish female, LTR for long-term relationship, NS for non-smoker... There are some ads so cleverly written that I knew I couldn't match. My favorite of all times is the one that says: "If I were laughter, I'd be warm, sensual, and spontaneous. If I were a car, I'd be a mini European import, filled with exciting travel plans. If I were a book, I'd be interesting, illustrated, and you'd curl up with me. If I were a recipe, you'd need quality ingredients and time to simmer and enjoy. If we are the ones for each other, we'll love and learn together for a long time. If I were you, I'd contact me. 62-72. NY & LI. NYRB Box 51307." And it ran for several months despite the rather expensive price ($5.85 per word), so the lady was financially secure to boot, or was she a material girl? Maybe I should have relied on some of my favorite air travel metaphors and told the truth: that I was afraid of flying solo, and taking off and landing, and crashing, and heaven only knows what else.

Finally I decided to try something simple for my own in *The New York Review of Books* online persona: "Merry widow, 63. European-born, American-educated college professor/writer. Tall, fetching, sassy, postmodern. Loves excitement of city life and peacefulness of nature. Seeks Philadelphia area, energetic, accomplished man 58-73, to share it all: arts, travel, politics, dining, and then some philawriter@gmail.com. "

My *Splenda* Daddy
For Bernard Stehle

Secretly I had always wished for a sugar daddy. Despite being an open feminist, I was in the closet, so to speak, about this fantasy. I wanted someone ten years older, at least, who, as a bonus, would make me look younger, now that I was fast passing middle age. Someone to dote on me, to treat me everywhere, to take me on a cruise and buy me a diamond ring. What the hell; even surprise me with a fur coat. Women who have sugar daddies, on principle, are not politically correct.

In the meantime, I was falling (didn't I know that love was a four letter word?) for another artsy type who looked older all right, but was just about my age. He was generous, that's true. If he had the money, he'd buy me a beautiful jewel, I was sure of that. But instead, he brought me a clear plastic bangle from South Street that looked like amber. The cruise was out of the question, while going to New York City on the Chinatown bus was certainly in the cards. And what about the fur coat? Couldn't he find it in one of the thrift shops we had visited, looking for Christmas presents? Turns out he called my bluff and told me that real feminists didn't wear furs.

But in his own way, he did dote on me. He found me lovely from the top of my auburn hair to my brightly painted toes. He didn't object to my peculiar Castilian accent or the occasional cultural gaffe. From the first day, he called and came when he said he would, even though he showed up *sans* wheels. He made little photo albums of our special dates for me. So what if we always went Dutch? Maybe he thought that this made him worldly and sophisticated. At least he was tall, something I yearned for, while sugar daddies are usually short and pudgy, I feared.

It ended up that, despite his height, he did watch his weight. He used 2% milk in his coffee, and never real sugar—it was bad for the colon he said—he preferred Splenda.

The Hispanic Maid

My new career officially started when I showed up in California with some rubber gloves, an apron and my recipes in the suitcase. My oldest daughter had been diagnosed with breast cancer early that year and I was there to help during her surgery and recovery. To have one's 56 year-old husband die of cancer was sobering enough, but to have my own daughter, who was only 41, diagnosed less than two years later, was unconceivable. Somehow, innocently on my part, I thought I had paid my cancer dues and my family would be vaccinated against that disease. Lightning doesn't strike twice, right? Wrong, it sure does, and here we all were again in emergency mode. Cooking and taking care of my twin granddaughters, who were not yet five years old then, was cathartic for me. I liked being busy and being there to see how Diana was feeling. To be involved in the everyday routine was easier than worrying about her in Philadelphia. I was more than glad to be useful to them in this traumatic, difficult time.

When I arrived that summer my daughter looked thin after several months of chemotherapy, but she was calm and stronger than I expected, facing her upcoming surgery. Before I arrived, Dwayne was, as always, the caretaker *par excellence.* He was in charge of the shopping, the cleaning, the laundry, the children's schedule and most of the cooking. As it had happened earlier with Peter, Diana had enough managing her illness, but she also taught full-time until a couple of months earlier. The twins, however, were the center of attraction, creating a whirlwind of activity and joyful commotion every minute of the day. Unfortunately, they had given up their naps months before and they didn't go to bed willingly or before ten o'clock in the evening, when the adults were ready to call it a day.

One of the first things Dwayne and I did together was to get the girls a haircut so they wouldn't give me a hard time when combing their beautiful, blond curls. Both chose a Karen Carpenter cut, because their father had introduced them to the old Carpenters' songs, which now were their favorite music in the car. By the time I was brave enough to drive on the Los Angeles freeways, I found out that they knew all the songs by heart and sang them in perfect stereo sound. When I accidently hit the wrong button and the songs played at random, they started to scream in their synchronized duo: "Not *Rainy Days and Sundays,* Mare. After *Sing a Song* comes *We've Only Just Begun!*" I had to pull off the road, call Dwayne, and play the CD the right and only way, in order to get them to settle down.

Early on during my stay, we decided that my major responsibility would be grocery shopping and cooking. As Diana said, I was the queen of the refrigerator. Dwayne would do the dishes, never mind the rubber gloves. He likes listening to NPR on the radio and that was the only time he had to himself in the small apartment. My other major occupation was chauffeuring the little princesses to and from summer camp and swimming lessons and taking them to the park afterwards.

Sierra Madre is the most idyllic little town imaginable. There is only one traffic light and two major roads full of coffee shops, health food stores, quaint little restaurants, quirky gift shops and several spas; it's all very Californian. The Sierra Madre Mountains, which can be seen from every street, serve as backdrop. Each year at Christmas time, truck loads of snow from the mountains are brought to the center of town to build a gigantic snowman. Thank goodness there is enough time for all the children to have their pictures taken, because the snow promptly melts and the next morning there is only a big puddle and some mittens left on the ground. Every time I visited I would look for things to criticize, hoping to influence my daughter and her family to move back East. Other than the unpredictable weather, there was nothing but charm. On one occasion though, I arrived during a forest fire and the heavy burnt smell permeated the town and leaked into the apartment. The sign indicating the level of fire danger up the canyon was plain scary, to say nothing about the threat of the end of the world with the next unscheduled earthquake. But it would take cancer to get them to move back home months later.

The neighborhood park in Sierra Madre is next to the Public Library and it's shaded by magnolia trees. The twins would take off running for the monkey bars as soon as we crossed the street. At that time, they didn't play with other children. They inhabited a world of their own, with their private never-ending chatter about some movie or cartoon character; they didn't live close to Hollywood for nothing. On the very first day I was in the park with them, a young mother approached me and commented how darling the twins were. As a proud grandmother I told her about their precocious musical and cinematographic vocabulary. Soon I realized that she thought I was the maid and I didn't even have my apron on! After all, didn't I speak with a Spanish accent, wasn't I a brunette, especially next to my blond grandkids? Just for fun I didn't let on about my identity and thus, the Hispanic maid was born, although I don't think it's so funny when my friends call me that. This is my own story to tell.

The fact is that, despite my hard-earned Ph.D., I would be a perfect domestic employee. My mother taught me how to clean at a very early age, although we had a live-in maid most of the time when I was growing up in Spain. During Franco's time, many young women moved to the cities from the impoverished rural areas to work as domestics and most families could afford them, even if, like us, they weren't by any means wealthy. Like any proper Spanish home, ours was cleaned every morning. Each bedroom was aired while the beds were made. Fresh air was more important than Lysol or any similar cleaning product. Each day the floors were mopped or swept and the furniture dusted. Each day of the week had a special protocol; I think Mondays was the laundry, Tuesdays the ironing, Wednesdays probably the bathrooms and I know that the sheets were changed at least once a week, unless someone was sick and then they were changed daily. My mother went to the market every single day but Sundays, when the shops were closed. She knew the time of the arrival of the fish and fruit trucks and she was there waiting to get the freshest produce.

When I had my own family in the States, I enforced the cleaning duties I learned in the Old World. I've been told that I ran a tight ship, and I know my daughters resented having more chores than the average American kid — Diana in particular. Perhaps that's why she is practically allergic to housework now. I really don't know how I did it without help; on top of the housekeeping, I managed to cook three meals a day, finish my undergraduate degree, a Masters and a Ph.D., while rearing a family. And all this before Trader Joe's with the prepared, inexpensive foods existed, another California invention. Even now, when I have a woman who comes to clean one day every other week, my cleaning expertise comes in handy. It definitely pays to show them that I know how's it's done. I may be a college professor and a writer, but I'm no princess and I can get my hands dirty with the best of them.

My status as the Hispanic maid was confirmed when my *"consuegra"* arrived to take me out on a Sunday afternoon. Let me explain what *consuegros* are. It's the relationship between in-laws when the children marry. I'm convinced that the term doesn't exist in English because the relationship doesn't exist either, but in Hispanic culture it's very important. The two sets of parents see each other socially and definitely during family gatherings. It's a way to keep up with your married children whether they want to or not; it's a *yenta* thing to do. Interestingly enough, *mekhutonim*, a similar concept to *consuegros,* exists also in Yiddish. In any case, in Spain the maids always went out with their buddies on Sunday afternoons. They also had Thursday afternoons free, but I guess, as a rookie maid, I didn't get that privilege yet.

Peter used to say that the twins had their perfect moments. He would have been very pleased to know that when he died, they named a star after him. Imagine my surprise when they told me one night when I couldn't get them to sleep: "Look, Mare, that's Pare's star... and there is John Lennon's and Karen Carpenter's." Their parents had taught them to name stars as a way to remember their favorite people who are no longer with us.

As a consequence of Peter's death, but particularly when Diana became sick, my own spirituality suffered a crisis. I was raised a Catholic, but my family wasn't religious at all. Back then, everyone in Spain was Catholic. I was baptized, confirmed, had my first Communion and even married my first husband in the church, but being a Catholic is a totally different matter in the States and I never joined a congregation here. There are two things I kept from my first marriage: my two daughters and the Episcopalian religion. It felt familiar enough and at the same time, it was much more liberal, with ordained women, black and gay ministers and all the prayers in the vernacular. It's as beautiful as the Catholic rites, without the guilt. Since Peter was Jewish, when we started to talk about marriage, we planned to have the ceremony in a synagogue, but as the time approached, I wanted to have a church wedding and we ended up marrying in the lovely Episcopalian church, Holy Trinity, on Rittenhouse Square in Philadelphia, even though a rabbi also joined in as part of the ceremony.

During Peter's illness, I attended church regularly, his name was said out loud during prayers and I was as close to a believer as I've ever been. At least I treasured the sense of community, even if I didn't believe that an omnipotent God created the world in seven days, and much less the sexist story of Adam and Eve. I believed that Christ existed and living a Christian, ethical life, made sense to me, not because it's the only way to live, but because it's the one I know well. At first I prayed every night for Peter's recovery and later—for a peaceful death. I fell asleep each night repeating my prayers in

Spanish only to wake up one day, sometime later, to find out about my daughter's diagnosis.

And what about heaven and hell, a topic so often discussed in Nuestra Señora del Loreto, the religious school I attended as a child? Now I've concluded that both are here on this earth in equal measures and I've had some of both. Thank goodness they've canceled limbo, where the non-baptized children were supposed to go, or my own innocent twin granddaughters would have ended up there. Maybe most of life is purgatory, since I think they haven't canceled that yet.

Being with the twins was mostly heavenly. They were taught to wait for an adult to hold their hands at every street crossing, but they would race each other, screaming and swaying like swallows, to every crossway. They loved speed; at the playground in the park they would run from the rocket to the flying cars and ask me to push them in the swings as fast and high as possible.

Although they are not identical, they are really a pair, but they don't like that most people can't tell them apart. Dinah was born first and is a little rounder than Djuna who is wiry, but very sure-footed. One day they fooled their teacher and played at being each other. Even though they knew it would get them in trouble. They had to confess at lunchtime, because Djuna was on a gluten-free diet and she didn't want to get sick. They leave notes for each other in the school lockers and then read them in the car, saying: "Oh, Dinah, you are the best," and "No, Djuna, you are the best." The day I left to go back to Philadelphia I found a note from them in my purse: "We love you, Mare" with a big heart for the verb and the R in Mare as a walking-stick figure.

There are different theories for their unusual names. Peter used to say that Dinah is the name of the girl in a song by Bing Crosby, *"Someone's in the Kitchen with Dinah?"* and Djuna is the name of the English writer Djuna Barnes. But according to my daughter, Dinah was the name of a long-time-ago slave on her father's side of the family and Djuna is a character in Woody Allen's film, *Everyone Says I Love You*. As far as the twins are concerned, the jury is still out.

The twins love films most of all, but they focus on the strangest details: the hyenas in *The Lion King*, the three blind mice in *Shrek 2* or Antonio Bandera's accent in the voice-over. Of course they have commented on my accent, too, like when I read them *The Big Hug*, hoping they would fall asleep. That didn't happen and they were wide awake when their parents arrived and, just by chance, I got caught chatting with my friend Bernard on my cell, talking about being demoted- from the Hispanic maid to the teenage baby sitter!

When my daughter was feeling up to going out of the house, we made a trip with the twins to the American Girl store at The Grove in downtown Los Angeles. It reminded me that in my childhood in Madrid there was a fabulous store on Serrano Street where they sold Mariquita Pérez dolls with every possible accessory, to match the life of a typical Spanish little girl. I remember the outfits, the luggage, the different wigs, even the jewelry, although I didn't own a Mariquita Pérez. I had a Gisela, a more modest version, who also dressed in matching clothes to mine, much as the American Girls dolls do now. In the LA store I was particularly taken by the historical reproductions; Kaya, an American native doll; Addy, an African American model; and Kanani, a Hawaiian version. There was even a Hispanic Girl doll named Josefina. But the twins only wanted horses, a palomino and a filly, from the American West tradition. Things have changed since then and now both have, not the American Girl twin sets, but identical miniature reproductions of themselves. The dolls have pink cowboy boots with matching hats, very much as Dinah and Djuna do, although they don't usually like to dress alike.

My favorite twin story is when one day they came out of the bathroom chanting: "Mare is in *The New Yorker*, Mare is in *The New Yorker*." Considering that having one of my stories published in the magazine's fiction section is one of my absolute life dreams, I almost had a heart attack, although it's been a while since I had sent them a piece. But there I was, on page 52, a black and white drawing of a woman, wearing an apron, a pan and cooking spoon in her hands, looking proudly at her six-burner Wolf stove with red knobs—the only minor difference being that I have a Thermador at home. Leave it to the daughters of a cartoonist to recognize the likeness of a person in a drawing as real as if it were a photograph, and they were not even four years old then. Of course, the scary part is that they had already identified me as a cook in the kitchen, well before the real Hispanic maid was named.

Now my two daughters and their families live on the same block in Narberth, a Main Line suburb of Philadelphia that is almost as charming as Sierra Madre, but without the mountains as the background. Diana calls her neighborhood "central casting," a sure sign that Hollywood is still in her heart. On Thursday afternoons, I pick up the three grandchildren at the bus stop and stay with them until their parents come home from work. We do their homework, and sometimes, if they let me, I teach them some Spanish, although they prefer French, which is the language they learn at school. Last year, on the very first day of school, a friendly neighbor approached me at the bus stop and shook my hand saying: "You must be the nanny."

"What do you know," I thought to myself, "I've just been promoted!"

Eating Alone[2]

Of all the adjustments I had to make as a new widow, eating alone is one of the most difficult. By the time my dear husband had gone, I was used to going out to the movies alone, driving at night, paying the bills, even sleeping alone. But the meals are the last vestiges of the marriage to go. Breakfasts are not so bad because I'm never hungry in the morning. It doesn't matter that I have been in this country for over fifty years, I still have a Spanish stomach and my breakfasts are definitely continental: a glass of juice, my vitamins and some yogurt and I'm off to the gym for the Pilates class. Lunches are the easiest; many days I meet friends, especially the still-married ones who don't want to leave their husbands alone at dinner time. If I'm at home at lunchtime, I eat while answering e-mail or between conference calls, doesn't everyone? Or maybe the married folks are still enjoying a nooner?

Dinners are another story for those who like me, chew their food slowly and won't think of eating standing up. I particularly like company when I have dinner. At first I found the perfect solution when I started having dinner during the NBC news with Brian Williams. I always had a soft spot in my heart for Tom Brokaw and when he was replaced I made my peace with his successor, but

---

[2] An earlier version of this chapter will appear in *Two-Countries: US Daughters and Sons of Immigrant Parents*, forthcoming. Edited by Tina Schumann.

despite his good looks, he isn't much of a conversationalist. Besides, when summer approaches I like eating somewhat later, again, in the Spanish mode. For a long while I had the perfect solution: I called my father as I sat down at the table. He always did all the talking anyway, he never asked me any questions, and he was a terrible listener. When I confessed to him that I was eating my dinner, he said I had no manners, talking with my mouth full, but I assured him that he hadn't let me say a word. *"Menos mal,"* he said, "Thank goodness."

Once my father was on to me and he knew he had *carte blanche* to speak without interruptions, he would wait faithfully for my call and reproach me when I would miss an evening without letting him know. He certainly was one of the most entertaining dinner partners I ever had, despite the distance or maybe because of it. I remember one of our last conversations before he stopped speaking to me all together. He went on in great detail how, as we age, food becomes much more important than sex. I almost choked on my tuna empanada right there and then. When I was growing up, he had never been one to explain the birds and the bees to his children. But now he was telling me that the libido fades sooner or later and besides, "who in the world has sex three times a day?" while food, he continued, was essential every day. That much I knew, my dad never missed a meal in his life and if he ever did, he would remind my mother for days, asking her to give him some extra bread or cheese because he hadn't had enough a few days before.

Yes, food was the all consuming topic growing up during the Franco years in Spain. My family fared well, thanks to some relatives in the countryside who brought extra eggs and sausages to Valencia. Lucky for us, we also had an uncle who owned a cheese importing business and he provided us with a care package, when we visited him every Sunday. It occurs to me now that perhaps we visited him so regularly to pick up the extra food. He was a bachelor who doted on the children of the family. My mother's main occupation was to walk on a daily basis from market to market in the city, looking for the best cuts of meat or fresh fish. She knew the delivery times at every spot and would address the merchants by their first names. I'm sure that the fact she was so good looking didn't hurt. Her main gripe was that coffee was so hard to find and she had to mix it half and half with chicory or even worse, do without on some days. I wasn't a big eater as a child, so I don't ever remember being hungry. My brother was a picky eater and things got worse when he saw a dead horse hanging in the butcher's shop. From that day on he wouldn't eat meat, a fact that worried my parents to no end; how would their first-born son achieve his full potential? Now it is true that I'm quite a bit taller than him, despite a very sweet tooth as my only eating accomplishment.

When we moved to Madrid, things got a little better. Although the city is farther from the sea, the fish that arrived at the local fish shop was fresher than in Valencia. My mother would be in line, promptly, at eleven. The main meal at two o'clock was always a fish dish: codfish Bilbao style, baked flounder, fresh sardines—my father's favorite. Dinner was something lighter, chicken or some kind of egg dish, served very late because my dad tutored students at home until at least ten in the evening. Meat was only served on holidays and other special occasions. The family packages didn't arrive as regularly in Madrid, but my father would occasionally receive a food basket from one of his private students and, at Christmas time, we often had a Serrano ham hanging in the pantry or a turkey waiting its execution in the laundry room.

I said that I was not a big eater, but I certainly had my favorites among my mother's recipes: *carne mechada* (stuffed flank steak) with tiny, square French fries, *patatas a cuadritos; pollo en escabeche* (stewed chicken in vinegar and pine nut sauce); baked macaroni with chorizo sausage; and, of course, dessert soufflé to appease my sweet cravings. Also, let's not forget the *paella valenciana*, my mother's signature dish. In addition to her looks, my father appreciated her cooking abilities. It wasn't unusual that he would show up for the main mid-day meal with an unannounced guest from the university— this was way before the era of cell phones or even pay phones—and he could count on my mother placing another setting at the table and having some delicious three course meal at the ready. I regret that I didn't learn to cook more from my mother, although she did send me, after I moved away and got married, some of her recipes, which I've kept to this day. She died much too soon, the same year as Franco (1975), although he really overstayed his welcome.

For a while after my husband died, I indulged in all my favorite foods: *pâtes*, cheeses, olives, potato chips, pasta, sausages, banana nut muffins, chocolate and all sort of candies from Trader Joe' eaten any time of day, without any rhyme or reason. Lucky for me I have a metabolism to match my energy and, anyway, this phase didn't last long. Soon I was back to my healthy Mediterranean diet, eating three times a day, albeit lonely at dinner time. And, as much as I hated to admit it, I missed Peter's cooking. He had his signature dishes, too: Russian Tea Room borscht, bouillabaisse, veal stew and most of all, my mother's *aioli* (garlic mayonnaise).

Let me explain how my mother's recipe got into Peter's hands when he didn't even get to meet her. When I was growing up *aioli* was made by hand with a mortar and pestle. My mother would not allow anyone to enter or exit the kitchen while she was making it. The windows had to be closed; a draft would certainly ruin the mayonnaise. When we moved to Madrid she complained for months until she got the hang of making it at the high altitude. I guess *aioli* works best at sea level. The strangest rule was that she couldn't have her period and make the mayonnaise at the same time, particularly since she was known for bleeding profusely. I got my first period late, not until I was fourteen but, unfortunately, I didn't care much for *aioli* before then and I never learned how to make it. After that, my brother was sure to say that I was menstruating as soon as the garlic and the olive oil appeared together on the kitchen counter. Under those circumstances no one wanted me around.

Peter was absolutely fearless, he also loved gadgets and I can attest that he never had a heavy period—*voilà,* the perfect combination! Our first Cuisinart came with a recipe for *aioli* and he could make it with the AC on, the overhead fan on, windows open or closed, whatever and wherever we were in relation to the ocean. Soon we were serving *aioli* with everything: steamed vegetables, lamb chops, shrimp, spread on French bread, even alongside the paella as they do in Barcelona, and I couldn't live without it. After he died I had the advantage of having gone through menopause, but I could still hear my mother's warnings about drafts and windows, so I didn't dare try to make it for many months. I was also so mad at Peter anyway for his betrayal that I didn't want to put anything in my mouth that reminded me of him. But little by little I started pleasuring my boyfriends and resurrecting his recipes.

Once I could make my own *aioli* I was unstoppable. Next I was cutting the breakfast grapefruit with the special knife as Peter used to do. I found his salad and soup cookbook and made a huge pot of borscht for a New Year's Day party; doubling recipes was something he didn't do, but following cooking instructions is not a must for me. Unfortunately I had already thrown away his favorite Creuset pot but I was craving his veal stew; no problem, now I have my own, bright orange Dutch oven and not only do I double, but even triple the mushrooms for the veal dish. The only recipe of his I haven't resurrected is the bouillabaisse, since we could never agree on the best version. His was tomato-based, which I considered gauche; I like the saffron-based kind, so I make my own version from the Monet recipes' cookbook.

I agree with my father, though. There is some correlation between food and sex. For me cooking with someone is like foreplay, all that bumping into each other in my tight galley kitchen. If I give him little bites of the food I'm tasting it's almost a given that I'll end up in bed with him. There is something very sensual about getting a hug from behind when I'm stirring the pasta and, if he gives me a soft kiss on the neck, it's bound to send a frisson down my back.

I often make paellas when I'm having a dinner party. For some reason my friends don't seem to tire of the old family recipe. For those occasions I cook it in the garden, on the Weber grill, even if we eat it indoors on my Talavera dishes. But if I cook a little *paellita* for a date with some quirky ingredient, cauliflower, for example, or whip up my own original XXI century gazpacho; then, watch out, I have my eye on that dude.

Not all the cooking expeditions end up well. I answered an ad in *The New York Review of Books* and a confirmed cook from Chicago came to spend New Year's Eve with me in Philadelphia. We went shopping for the detailed ingredients for his recipes of cod fish Callaloo and smoked salmon with curried potatoes at the famous Reading Market. The place was mobbed; we were not the only ones cooking at home for the holiday. He found everything on his list, including coconut milk and Jamaican spices I had never used before. Despite the cold, we walked back with our shopping bags full, something that always reminds me of being in Madrid; a good omen perhaps?

No. He was a very messy cook, not an ideal aphrodisiac for me. Turns out that he learned to cook aboard some merchant ship and he was used to throwing the stuff on the floor faster than I could wash the dishes, clean the counters and mop the floor. I wasn't a happy scullery maid... Needless to say, we never made it to the bedroom together.

Despite being a sailor, he was also a gentleman and I acted like a lady, too. We even stayed friends for a while and we spoke on the phone up to the time when I met Philip, the last person to answer my own ad in *The New York Review of Books*.

The recipes

Carne mechada (stuffed flank steak)

Every family in Spain has its own version of this dish. It also goes by the name of *matahambre* (kill the hunger). It can be stuffed with just about anything you have in the refrigerator or whatever is in season. My mother usually used colorful ingredients (carrots, eggs, celery, pickles) in order to have the meat slices look beautiful in addition to being flavorful.

Ingredients
2 ½ lb. flank steak
Two-egg omelet
Two carrots
Two celery stalks
Six cornichons
Six pitted black olives
Three slices of Jamón Serrano
Salt and pepper
3 TBS olive oil
3 TBS unsalted butter
1 cup beef broth
Method
Prepare the omelet, cooked with some parsley.
Peel carrots and slice thin length-wise, same with the celery, cornichons and olives.
Pound and roll out the steak until it is ¼ inch thick or less.
Arrange the other ingredients prettily and evenly on the meat.
Roll it carefully, don't worry if some of the ingredients escape.
Tie the roll with cooking string.
Season with salt and pepper.
Warm up the butter and oil until bubbly.
Sautee the meat carefully on all sides until browned evenly.
Turn heat down, cover with the beef broth and simmer until cooked through, for about half an hour.
Cool for fifteen minutes before cutting it in ½ inch slices.
Serve with any kind of potatoes or white rice and *aioli* on the side.

Abuelita's aioli (garlic mayonnaise)

Don't worry about the climate or anything else. This recipe is really fool-proof. Just refrigerate for a while if it seems a little runny.

Ingredients
1 egg plus 1 yolk
¼ tsp Dijon style mustard
¼ tsp salt
2 TBS fresh lemon juice
1 cup olive oil
3-4 garlic cloves, crushed, or some garlic powder
Method
Mix first four ingredients in small Cuisinart or blender for a few minutes.
Add oil gradually and continue beating until thickened and silky.
Add garlic and blend.
Serve cold. It keeps refrigerated for two to three days.

Baked macaroni with chorizo sausage

This was my brother's all-time favorite dish. My mother made it often, since he was such a picky eater. I didn't love it until it became my own kids' favorite and now the grandchildren ask for it, too. It seems to fulfill any child's appetite on both sides of the Atlantic.

Ingredients
1 lb macaroni
2 TBS olive oil
1 tsp pepper corns
3 bay leaves
1 lb lean ground beef

½ lb chorizo or pepperoni
1 large jar of spaghetti sauce
1 cup warm water with 2 beef cubes
Italian seasoning, salt and pepper
3 TBS butter
½ cup grated parmesan cheese
Method
     Cook pasta according to package instructions with olive oil, pepper corns and bay leaves.
Drain and arrange in baking dish.
Heat oven to 400°
Sautee ground beef with chorizo cut in small pieces.
Add tomato sauce, water and beef cubes. Simmer until creamy.
Pour tomato and beef mixture over macaroni.
Top with butter in small bits and parmesan cheese.
Bake 30 minutes until browned.

Dessert soufflé

My mother sent me this recipe in a letter, written in red ink in her curly, girly handwriting. It's a miracle that it's still legible, because she used airmail paper. It must have been close to the Christmas holidays, since she admonishes me to get going and try it a few times before my in-laws came for dinner. The fact is, I was always a bit afraid to make it. The business of setting the cognac on fire and bringing the flaming soufflé into the dining room can be intimidating. My mother was very brave and she served it every Sunday, whether it was Christmas season or not.

Ingredients
3 egg whites separated from its yolks
½ cup powdered sugar
1 cup regular sugar
3 TBS cognac or brandy
Graham crackers optional

Method
Mix the yolks with the regular sugar to form a crust on the bottom of the soufflé dish
Beat egg whites until peaks form, blend in powdered sugar. Pour carefully over yolk mix.
Bake at 275° in center of oven until lightly brown, about 10-15 minutes.

Pour cognac on the sides and light it as you bring it to the table. Make sure to blow it out quickly before the whole thing burns down!
You may substitute crushed Graham crackers for the crust instead of the egg yolks.

Concha's paella valenciana

When I was growing up in Spain, paellas were well known only in the Mediterranean regions of Valencia and Cataluña. According to my father, paellas were originally cooked outdoors over a fresh cut wood fire. Imagine his surprise when paellas started to be served in every restaurant in Madrid! My family never ate paella outside our home, unless we were in Valencia and we could go to La Marcelina at the beach. My version works well in the United States. I still never eat paella in a restaurant.

Ingredients
6 tablespoons olive oil
1 onion, chopped
1 green pepper, chopped
1 ripe tomato, chopped
3 garlic cloves, minced
1 lb Spanish chorizo or spicy Italian sausage, cut in small pieces
¾ lb. shrimp
½ lb. squid, cleaned (no ink)
¾ lb. fish (cod, sea bass, monk or any other solid white fish)
2 lb. mussels

1 cup white wine
lemon, herbs
1 ½ cups rice (Uncle Ben's Converted)
1 four ounce jar of red pimientos, cut in thin strips
1 cup frozen peas
    For the broth: 3 cups water, 3 fish bouillon cubes, ½ tsp saffron, 1 tsp parsley flakes, salt & pepper
Method
Steam mussels in white wine, lemon and your favorite herbs.
Discard top shell and set aside.
Prepare broth in a small sauce pan, simmering water with seasonings.
Heat oil in paella pan and sauté chorizo with vegetables.
Add fish, squid and shrimp and sauté all together five more minutes.
Add rice, mix well and add simmering broth to cover.
Top with pimientos and peas.
    Cook at low heat on range top until most of broth has disappeared, 15-20 minutes. Finish cooking in a 350° oven fifteen minutes more.
    Add mussels on top right before serving.
    Can be kept warm in oven (turned off), covered with aluminum foil.

Russian Tea Room hot borscht

    In my years as a shiksa, I prepared this dish often. In fact, I still like to make it every New Year's Day, when I have an open house for friends and family coming to Philadelphia for the Mummer's Parade. I leave it on the stove, simmering all afternoon, and serve it with pumpernickel bread and fresh butter.

Ingredients
1 cup finely chopped carrots
1 ½ cups finely chopped onions
1 ½ cups finely chopped celery

1 ½ cups finely chopped parsnips
1 can of beets, chopped
2 TBS butter
3 cups beef or vegetable broth
1 ½ cups finely shredded cabbage
1 ½ cups drained canned tomatoes, chopped
Salt and freshly ground black pepper
Sour cream
Snipped fresh dill
 Method

In a large soup pot barely cover the carrots, onions, celery and parsnips with boiling water and boil them gently, covered for 20 minutes.

Add the beets, butter, broth, cabbage, tomatoes and salt and pepper to taste and boil 15 minutes more.
Serve hot, garnished with a dollop of sour cream and dill.

Can be doubled, tripled, however many people you need to feed. This recipe is enough for 8 servings.

Peter's veal stew

I used to love coming home and smelling this dish cooking! The curry would permeate the entire kitchen and linger all evening. Be careful with the discarded *bouquet garni*, though; Casey, our beagle, got hold of it one time and made an awful mess all over the kitchen floor and dining room rug.

Ingredients
2 TBS olive oil
2 lbs veal, cut into cubes
2 onions, finely chopped
2 garlic cloves, finely chopped
2 carrots, cut into 1" pieces
2 stalks celery, cut into 1" pieces
2 TBS flour
1 ½ TBS curry powder

1 cup white wine
1 cup chicken broth
Bouquet garni: 3 stalks parsley, 1 bay leaf, 1tsp thyme, 1 TBS peppercorns
2 TBS butter
1 jar small white onions, drained
½ lb of mushrooms, cut into quarters
Method
Heat the oil in a skillet. Add a few cubes of veal at a time and brown them on all sides.
Transfer the veal to a casserole.
Fry onions, garlic, carrots and celery in the same oil in the skillet for 5 minutes.
Stir in the flour and curry powder and cook for 1 minute. Stir in the wine.
Transfer all the ingredients to the casserole.
Add the chicken broth and *bouquet garni*.
Bake covered in a 350° oven for 1 hour and 10 minutes until the veal is very tender.
Discard the *bouquet garni* and refrigerate overnight.

When ready to serve, bring to room temperature and heat casserole on top of stove.
Heat remaining butter in skillet and sauté the small onions and mushrooms until brown.

Add onions and mushrooms to veal casserole.

When it reaches boiling point, cover and place in a 350° preheated oven for 20 minutes.

Monet's bouillabaisse

This dish has a painter's name because of its beautiful golden color and it should be served in some special wide pasta bowls to show it off appropriately. This is my answer to Peter's traditional red bouillabaisse, which I never tried to make.

Ingredients
1 lb dry salt cod, cut in small pieces
2 cups olive oil
1 ½ cup flour
6 potatoes, peeled and sliced
4 leeks, white part, sliced
½ tsp pepper
¼ tsp ground cloves
2 garlic cloves, minced
2 TBS parsley
1/8 tsp saffron
1 bay leaf
6 cups chicken or fish broth
Method
Soak dry cod in water for at least 12 hours, changing the water three or four times. If cod is very salty, soak longer time.

Pat dry cod and coat with flour on all sides. Reserve leftover flour.

Fry cod pieces in a Dutch oven pot, and put aside.

Fry potatoes in the same oil and put aside

Discard most of the oil, leaving only 3 TBS, and sauté the garlic and the leeks.

Add spices, leftover flour and broth, add potatoes and simmer for 15 minutes.

Slide cod pieces gently into broth. Simmer for 5 more minutes.

Serve with toasted French bread and aioli on the side.

Concha's XXI Century gazpacho

Gazpacho means simply "cold soup" and although the traditional tomato version is still popular, any variation with fruits and/or vegetables is desirable in a contemporary Spanish menu. As a post-modern widow, I made this recipe up, deconstructing the Italian melon and prosciutto antipasto.

Ingredients
1 honeydew melon, chilled
2 slices French bread
Fresh basil and mint
½ cup of olive oil
¼ cup white balsamic vinegar
6 cornichons
Salt and pepper
6 slices of prosciutto
Method
Soak bread in cold water.
Cut melon in small pieces, discarding seeds and rind.
Puree in blender all ingredients, except prosciutto, in two batches.
Chop prosciutto for garnish.
Serve cold, garnished with prosciutto, as a first course or appetizer
It may also be served cold as an *hors d'oeuvre* in tequila glasses as an *amuse-bouche*

Smoked salmon with curried potatoes

This recipe is the legacy of the sailor-cook. Each boyfriend should leave at least one recipe for a widow's repertoire.

Ingredients
¾ lb of salmon
½ cup olive oil
4 small onions, minced
½ head of garlic cloves, minced
6 small potatoes, thinly sliced
1 can coconut milk
1 TBS curry powder
Method
Grill or sauté salmon and set aside.
Sauté onions and garlic in olive oil. Add potatoes.

Add coconut milk and curry. Simmer until done. Consistency should be like scalloped potatoes.

Place salmon on top gently, just to warm it up. Salmon should float.

Serve with an exotic bread (Blue Mountain Country Bread or Jamaican Curry, for example) and unsalted butter.

Making Magic In Montalcino

I often think how Peter created magic around him. He had a way of turning an ordinary day into something special, a routine task into a funny event, a sad moment into a memorable one, like the time he organized a walk through Old City in Philadelphia on a snowy night for out-of-town guests. For some reason this was especially true during trips or maybe I remember this ability of his during my own travels. No wonder I dread flying solo almost as much as eating alone.

After Peter died, I took a couple of journeys with girlfriends, but despite years of friendship, we ended up irritating each other, and I even lost some friends in the process. We all know how difficult it is to find a good traveling companion, almost as difficult as finding a good partner. I also traveled with occasional boyfriends and, unfortunately, traveling only accelerated what was probably going to end up badly anyway. So this time I decided to embark alone. My first solo destination was Tuscany, perhaps not the best choice, since I had traveled there with Peter the very year we met.

Peter and I were leaving a Hispanic Literature Conference, which was held in a restored monastery in Pastrana, about thirty kilometers outside Madrid. We had rented a Ford Fiesta that had the hiccups in the lower gears, or was it that Peter was having trouble with the clutch? I didn't dare ask since, despite my pride at being the European, I never learned how to use a stick shift. With his customary spontaneity, Peter asked:

"Would you like to go to Italy?" And we were off.

The first few days of that memorable journey were just a lot of driving with the occasional tasty tapas or bouillabaisse up the Costa Brava, the French Mediterranean coast through Marseille, on to Nice, crossing into Italy by the Alps. Despite its elegant Duomo, Milan failed to impress me until Peter walked me, without even checking a map, to the Convent of Santa Maria delle Grazie. Seeing "The Last Supper" live for the first time sent a frisson down my lapsed Catholic back. How many other girlfriends had Peter taken to this magical spot?

In Venice, some of his old guitar friends had made reservations for us in a romantic place overlooking the Grand Canal. I won't give Peter credit for this since he didn't find it himself and the shower water was barely lukewarm. But he certainly scored again when he insisted that we check out what was playing in La Fenice. *Don Quichotte* by Massenet, two tickets in a center box, that very evening, consider it done. He even knew to buy some chocolate to eat during the performance, like Italians do, and we were having a pizza afterward exactly where the cast stopped for a bite to eat. Program signed by the soprano, no problem.

Fiesole, outside Florence, was another success. Not only was the view of the city spectacular from the hotel veranda, where we were having our cappuccinos, but it was much cooler and less crowded than the center of the city below us. That is until a line of traffic started forming up the hill and our supposed peaceful hotel became attacked by a beehive of Fiats and Citroëns looking for a parking spot. The waiter explained to us that there was a performance at the old Roman theater behind us.

"Let's take a look," Peter said immediately.

It was a live version of the ballet *Blood Wedding* by Antonio Gades, which had just been released as a film by Carlos Saura. Now imagine how the Spaniard and the professor in me felt! I was planning to teach Lorca's play of the same title, comparing it to the film in the upcoming semester. How was this possible? The wooden planks of the stage were surrounded by almost perfect Ionic columns and other artifacts. I'm sure the seats of the amphitheater facing the stage had been reconstructed, small cushions covered the antique stone. Ruins of sculpture and ornamental details were all around us as if designed by a postmodern wizard. As the evening turned into night, camouflaged lights would appear. I couldn't decide whether to watch the ballet or luxuriate in the surroundings.

They say that smell is the most lasting sense we posses. Peter surprised me with a jasmine bouquet in Portofino, our last stop before we boarded El Canguro ferry in Genova back to Spain, saying:

"I just want you to know that, if you weren't married already, I'd marry you right now."

How is that for a promising line for a newly separated lady traveler? The pungent, sweet smell of the pseudo-bridal bouquet stayed with me the rest of that trip. Never mind that it was the first day of Ramadan and hundreds of Muslims were going back to Mecca, which left us without even a *poltrona* reservation to sit on. No worries, we just played casino all the way to Barcelona on top our suitcases, sitting on a corner of the deck. He probably beat me at every game and I probably didn't even mind.

The smell of jasmine was one of the first impressions I had when I arrived in Rome last summer, but I tried to ignore it and stop thinking about the past; let's concentrate on my new life. An advantage of having been to China and India recently is that flights to Europe seem so short now. Another plus is that I've discovered Tylenol PM and I sleep through the flight; I don't even feel jet lagged. But I didn't have to wait long for my first travel mishap. When I arrived at L'Hotel Cinquantatre my room "was not ready."

"No problem, I'll leave the suitcases here and tour around a bit," I said, being a good sport, when we all know how nice it is to get to one's room after an overnight flight.

"No, it won't be ready over the entire weekend, it has a leak and a broken pipe in the bathroom."

I was suspicious of Eurobookings already and this just confirmed it. Nima, the concierge (notice that I was already on a first name basis, surely a good sign), surprised me by telling me that he had booked "a much better room at a much better place." He would call a taxi, pay the driver and, by the way, my new room was ready. What could have been a travel disaster, turned out to be a great experience, since Domus Australia is a charming boutique hotel, centrally located near Termini Station.

The next stop of my travels as a woman alone was Montalcino, where I was attending a writers' workshop. If it wasn't because our teacher warned us not to use the word "quaint," I would say that it is one of the quaintest spots I have ever visited (there goes my A in the course). The narrow stone walks meandering up and down the Tuscan hills, the open vistas of the vineyards from every corner, the songs of the birds in Italian, all created an aura of enchantment.

On the very first evening, after a wonderful Brunello wine tasting in the Fortezza, I saw a small theater nestled behind the Piazza del Popolo. An abstract sculpture graced the entrance area, contrasting with the old stone walls. On a tiny marquis there was an announcement of the evening's performance: *L'opera degli straccioni*, a concert performance based on *The Threepenny Opera* by Bertolt Brecht, sung in Italian, was being performed in thirty minutes. I quickly talked other participants into joining me—two other women traveling alone. We bought a box on the first row of the balconies. There was a short wait in the cozy lobby. Families with children were waiting dressed up in stylish linen and a touch of punk. Young, artistic-looking men, all in black, stood outside inhaling the last puff of their cigarettes.

Going inside I felt like Alice in Wonderland—I'm tall and the hall was so small. The three of us barely fit into the tiny box seats.

Frescoes graced the ceiling and a modest chandelier hung in the center. There were two tiers of box seats decorated with gold and burgundy accents. The orchestra seats filled up slowly, people meandered about greeting their friends. The lights turned off almost thirty minutes late. Stereotypes aside, the Italians can't talk about the Spaniards' punctuality.

The fifteen piece orchestra, L'Orchestra della Filarmonica Giacomo Puccini, all in trendy black, paraded out first. There were mostly wind instruments, with only one string, a guitar and banjo player, a piano and percussion. The fourteen voices of the choir, Gruppo Polifonico Giacomo Puccini, quickly followed. I noticed immediately that they were mostly senior people, probably local talents. Although they were also dressed in classic black, there were touches of bright color, some bright aqua eye glasses, and a woman with lipstick-red hair. When the opera singers, seven men and seven women, marched out, the audience broke into an applause that lasted until the maestro emerged in the pit and bowed.

I'm not sure that Peter would have liked this Italian version of *The Threepenny Opera*. It certainly wasn't a classic performance, but rather a postmodern one. Each singer, striking in their individuality, carried a simple prop: a bright foulard or a fur stole for the prostitutes, a kinky hat for the wife and daughter, police batons for the constables, guns for the gangsters and tattered scarves for the beggars. The music was jazzy and loud, especially "Mack the Knife," the song now made famous by the likes of Bobby Darin, Louie Armstrong, Ella Fitzgerald and Frank Sinatra.

At that very moment, I became aware that I was having a wonderful time. It wasn't La Fenice, but it certainly had its charm. I was not with Peter, but I didn't feel lonely. I just had to stop gazing at happy-looking couples and remembering my trips with him. The fact is that I can get used to traveling alone. I can speed through as many museums as I want, since I've been told that I march in life as if I were on roller skates. I can over plan, overspend, oversleep, over pack and overdress. I can get lost, read a map wrong and find my way back to the hotel anyway. I can flirt, even pick up some local Adonis, although I haven't tried that yet, but I better keep away from another musician... and I know that my mind is wandering from *The Three Penny Opera* while Jenny is singing about her lost love, Mackie Messer, a scoundrel-like character as Peter was. The most important discovery is that I realized I'm the one making my own magic now.

The next morning, although it was unusually rainy for that time of year in Tuscany, I took a walk up to the center of town during one of our workshop's breaks. I couldn't believe my eyes. Who was coming toward me was none other than Brown La Tigre, the chief of police from the opera. I wasn't about to miss a chance to introduce myself to him.

"Mr. Brown, Mr. Brown," since I didn't know his real name, I said loudly.

And he turned around immediately.

"I saw the opera last night. It was wonderful, *bellissima,* so much so that I'm writing a piece about it... Would you mind having your picture taken with me, as souvenir?"

"*Piacere.* I would be happy to," said Giovanni Guerrini in his best English, introducing himself and kissing my hand. Magical!

The Matchmaker. Desencuentros

Let's face it, we would all like to meet someone cute, someone sitting next to us on a plane or a train like in a movie—think of *Before Sunrise*. I have my own fantasy; I see a gorgeous, tall man who looks familiar at a writers' conference and he starts coming toward me saying in a foreign accent "You look familiar, have we met before?" Trite, I know, but oh so perfect! But when all else fails, when we have tried several Internet sites, when we have placed an ad in *The New York Review of Books* and have answered a few of them as well, when our friends and relatives have introduced us to several suitable acquaintances and we have tried to strike up a conversation in airports, supermarkets, local bookstores and just about everywhere we go, there is always the matchmaker.

Yes, I'm not inventing this, a matchmaker, like in an old-fashioned film, say *Fiddler on the Roof* or *Crossing Delancey*. George, from my Pilates class, told me about her. I tried to hush him up, embarrassed to death that our teacher would hear him in the one place where I haven't made it obvious that I'm on the prowl. He couldn't say enough good things about Jo. She was lovely, so knowledgeable and courteous. With such a high recommendation, I jotted her number down on my gym membership card. She hadn't yet given me her charming pink business card with a gold heart in the middle.

I drove to her place in suburban Philadelphia, a few exits off US 95 North from the center of town. Her tiny office walls were covered with pictures of happy, smiling couples just like an OBGYN doctor has hers covered with adorable babies. Jo was so chatty and friendly that I wondered if she had met her husband as a client. She kept saying how nice my skin was and how young I seemed—I shouldn't tell my age to anyone—that I looked at least ten years younger. How was I not to like her? She wasn't cheap, but gave me an introductory price of $200.00, perhaps given my lovely skin. That fee was good for two months and guaranteed four matches.

Going to a matchmaker, just like joining a new website, helps one focus. "What exactly do I want in a partner?" Jo asked. First of all, he has to be accomplished, cultured, attractive, energetic, financially conservative and politically liberal. He must want to travel. Of course he will be kind, pleasant, good company and all the usual social requirements. My therapist says that I'm not demanding, but that, since I have lots to offer, I want lots in return. Maybe I'll have to lower my expectations if I ever want to find a mate.

Since I like to make a research project out of everything, I had some questions of my own for Jo: Who are her typical clients, how does she meet them, are the women happy with her services? Turns out that she has been in business for more than twenty years, and she advertises in the local press and on dating sites, but most of her men and women come referred by someone else. "No, they are not desperate," Jo assures me, they are all professionals, like me, and they just don't have time to waste on the Internet.

But, just like in a dating site, there was a protocol to follow. I would get a phone call from the men first. "Don't expect to talk too long; men hate chatting on the phone," Jo said. If it goes well, then a short date is set for coffee or an after-work drink. No one wants to spend time and money on dinner if there isn't chemistry, a word she used often, making her service sound more like science than magic. She expected a call with my first impressions after the initial meeting and then we were on our own.

I've done some matchmaking myself, with little success I might add. I have been known to fix my ex-boyfriends with some of my own girlfriends. I think of it as a way to soften the blow, if I was the one who initiated the breakup. But, for some reason, the guys get touchy about this and by the time they make the contact I'm not even sure it was a good idea. Like the time I suggested to a Rutgers University professor, who loved his Maltese puppies, he would like to meet Mary, who was crazy about her Dalmatians. I'm not sure if he didn't like her or her dogs. I also fixed Mary up with Charlie, a tango instructor, since she loves ballroom dancing. I don't know what happened, but that was a fiasco, too, and I retired from the business of meddling in my friends' love lives.

Jo fixed me up right away with three men and, she was right, their phone conversations were indicative of what there was to come. In fact, Jack and I never made it beyond the first phone conversation. Jack admitted that he hadn't been in Philadelphia since the fifties and didn't like it anyway. I said that he didn't even know the city; it has changed so much in the last six decades! No wonder he mentioned Famous Deli as a good place to meet, which is about the oldest, most stuffy place to eat off South Street, while I was thinking of one of the many trendy places I'm familiar with, like Amada or Garces Trading Company.

He also told me he had written a memoir of his Italian family and their move to New York City. The unbelievable part is that, even though it hadn't been published, it had been picked up by a director and it was being made into a film. Saying that I was envious doesn't even come close to how I felt. The producers had given him a Lexus (he usually drove a Ford Taurus) and a credit card, so he could go from his Southern Jersey home to the big city to be a consultant. He couldn't take me out yet, because they were filming in New York, and on the first snowy day he would have to leave immediately to shoot the outdoor scenes. All this conversation took place in what I would call immigrant volume. I remember how my family screamed on the phone when they used to call from Spain before the days of Skype. "Helloooo," Jack would say and, without meaning to, I would answer "Whaaaat?" in a very loud voice. I never heard from him again.

The first man I met through Jo was Pietro, also an Italian, this one from South Philly. He was as good-looking as she mentioned, dressed all in black, with a tight muscle shirt to show off his physique. He smelled good, too. Come to think of it, all of Jo's men smelled delicious. His best feature was his silver hair, sleeked back with lots of product, framing his handsome face and his eyebrows, which were shaped like upside down Vs. Think of Rocky Balboa without the broken nose. Unfortunately he was covered with gold jewelry: a big watch, a thick chain bracelet and most prominently, an elaborate crucifix, hanging from a gold chain, in the middle of his powerful chest. There was no doubt that Pietro was more handsome than I'm pretty, and I'm no wall flower. He spoke with a South Philly accent, which is funny if you hear it on a TV or radio ad, but is very embarrassing if you are in a sophisticated Society Hill bar and one of your neighbors is right behind him. Luckily, my neighbor was not with his wife, so he also pretended not to see me.

This Italian jock had never been out of the country; the only time he had been on a plane, he went to Florida. He admitted that he would need to be sedated to get airborne again. As I've said before, I won't go to bed with Republicans, but this guy probably didn't even vote. He was incensed when he heard that I had been to Cuba with my students and had loved my recent trip to China. "What are you, a Communist?" he said gesturing with his hand under the chin. No, he didn't go to movies. No, he didn't know Italian, although he spoke with his hands and showed me some not so nice gestures. How's that for a match?

We spoke about our children. His daughter was a waitress and his son already had his own heating and air-conditioning business. And there I was telling him that not everyone needs to go to college. If either one of my daughters could hear me now! At that point he told me how perceptive he was and how no one could BS him. What a good time we were having and how much he wanted to see me again! He couldn't wait to make some of his mother's spaghetti with traditional gravy for me—that's the word for sauce in South Philly.

What was I to do? I told Jo the truth: that physically Pietro was very attractive, but that he wasn't my type and that I could never take him home to meet my children.

Steven, a retired corporate man, also dressed in black, was my next match. His hair was perfect as well. I started to wonder if Jo had a dress code for her male clients. I made the mistake of dressing conservatively with a matching outfit that made me look like an Iberian Airlines flight attendant, without the white gloves and the box hat, because despite his business career Steven was a biker now and there were his helmet and leather jacket to prove it. That would teach me to dress to please my date.

Our conversation started well enough. At least he had made money from his real estate investments and I love talking about the ups and downs in the real estate market. But then, I don't know how, *The Bible* made an unscheduled appearance and he was telling me that marriage was supposed to be between a man and a woman only, period. Appearances can be so deceiving; despite being Jewish, Jo attracted conservative Catholic men and, despite my goody-two-shoe clothes, I was a Communist and a radical.

Again, I called Jo immediately and told her that Steven and I weren't a good match, only to find out that he had already called her and told her that there was no chemistry between us. Put that in your pipe and smoke it, Concha. And here I had painted my nails a provocative deep red—something I hadn't done in decades, certainly not for a date, maybe for a fund-raiser gala someplace.

James, however, took the cake. He was one of the most unpleasant dating experiences I have ever had. He was talkative on the phone, although there were plenty of red flags: this country is toxic, his sister is also toxic, his brother's children are toxic. He described himself as a European because he had lived in Paris for a period of time (not). He did have an interesting career. He was a physician with his own practice that specializes in curing cancer with intravenous doses of vitamin C, although I had never heard of that kind of experimental treatment.

Setting up a date with James was a complicated affair. He was a vegetarian, so we couldn't meet at a Jewish deli I suggested (as if they didn't serve salads there). We met at a Starbucks at 12:30 PM, which I thought meant lunch. But when he arrived a few minutes late, I might add, he didn't want anything, because he had already drank a protein smoothie somewhere and I had to buy my own sandwich and drink. No problem. From the very beginning, the conversation was strained and his toxicity list had grown to include some of his patients and friends. I changed the subject to traveling, mentioning some of the study tours I had taken with my students to South America, Cuba and South Africa…

"Oh, paid vacations," he said. I thought he was kidding, so I laughed, but he was serious. When I mentioned that perhaps he said that because he never had children; traveling with fifteen or twenty teenagers is never a vacation, he said that he was offended, got up and left. I sat there eating my sandwich alone, shaking in my seat. Being left in a coffee shop, that was a first. This time, I told Jo that I was taking a leave of absence and that I wanted to take a break from dating. I didn't mention to her how I missed using Google to find out information about perspective dates and how much better it is to communicate on e-mail for a while before having to pay for one's lunch.

Several months later, out of the blue, Jo called me up with another possible match. I think she felt badly about my last one and I was again between boyfriends, so I agreed to try one more time. Dating is like childbirth; you forget how painful it is and you end up trying again. Clark worked around the corner from my home, so we could meet very easily. He was younger than me, but as young as I looked Jo was sure it didn't matter. This time a happy hour meeting at a trendy new place, The Red Owl Tavern, was set effortlessly. Clark was not Superman, but he was also attractive, blond and dressed casually with a Hawaiian shirt and khakis. He had never been married, lived on the same street where he grew up in suburban Philadelphia. No, he didn't come to the city on weekends, since he was there every weekday for work. No, he didn't see foreign movies. No, he didn't care for the opera, the orchestra or the ballet. His favorite activity was playing Trivial Pursuit on weekends with a so-called "meet-up" group (I made a mental note not to ever try that possibility).

This time I felt guilty calling Jo with the bad news; Clark was such a nice guy. I kept thinking of a Spanish word I haven't been able to translate into English, *desencuentro*. The trusty Google dictionary says that it is a "disagreement," a "misunderstanding," a "failure to meet up," a "mix-up," and "unmeeting," (is there such a word?). But none of these do justice to this Spanish concept. Literally it means an "un-encounter." Let me illustrate it. A *desencuentro* is when two people would have never met had it not been for an introduction by a well-meaning matchmaker. A *desencuentro* is when two people would be on a different time zone even if they live in the same city, like Clark and I. Not surprisingly, when Clark called Jo with his report, he told her that I was delightful, but I seemed "a little long in the tooth." How's that for an apt American expression?

Into The Woods

This is not a fairy tale, so don't expect a traditional happy ending. The closest I came to finding my charming prince was when Philip Bertocci answered my ad in *The New York Review of Books.* We even lived together for a year, but not happily ever after. We are still good friends and we go out, visit each other, take occasional trips together, although any mention of making our relationship more permanent sends him into panic and retreat. He's over seventy years old and has never been married. What was I thinking? He warned me from the start. He didn't bond easily. His real bonds are his three siblings, his youngest sister in particular. In fact, she keeps the engagement ring their mother saved for Philip to give to his beloved some day. Good luck with that!

On paper Philip and I are a good match. We are both tall, thin and in good physical shape. We love the arts; he leans toward painting, I prefer the cinema. We are altruistic, liberal and compassionate. We have the same internal clock, not night owls, like a typical Spaniard, nor larks, as older people tend to become. We are very civilized; up by eight, in bed by midnight. Very important, we both have similar energy levels. He's one of the few people I know who can walk faster than I do. I don't have to worry that I'm going to give him a heart attack while I'm strolling through the streets in Old City Philadelphia. However, here come the differences. He's rather introspective and a loner, while I'm very social and outgoing. He's old fashioned; he tells me that I have "a bee in my bonnet" and that I "float his boat," while I label myself "*una chica moderna,*" (particularly since taking my iPad to bed). Our biggest conflict is (and here is where we get into trouble) that I'm generous to a fault, due to my own insecurities, so he tells me, while he is Spartan. Like a good New Englander, Philip conserves his money, his words, his feelings. He dispenses love as if it were in an eye-dropper.

Philip has the perfect pedigree to match my own and then some: doctorate in European Studies from Yale, taught at Stanford before switching to a career in law, with a degree from The University of Pennsylvania. He was a public advocate in a non-profit until he retired, reluctantly, after more than thirty years. He stills goes to his old office regularly on a volunteer basis, no more paychecks. He speaks French fluently, but for some reason refuses to study Spanish and once he says no to something, he rarely changes his mind.

Philip is definitely miscast in the role of a prince, although he has his perfect moments, particularly while he is in Vermont, where his family owns a second home. I've gone up there with him many times. He grows Christmas trees as a hobby. Through the dining room window you can see them standing tall in many sizes across the field. Behind the line of trees, there are the Green Mountains with Mount Elmore and Mount Mansfield visible on clear days, all the way to the horizon. I have sat writing at the dining room table and I have watched Philip run around his trees, wearing some old T-shirt and worn-out jeans, pruning here and there, but keeping the natural look of the place. Neat rows of balsam firs are not for him. At dinner time, we watch the sunset progress from fluorescent light to salmon strips to darkness framed by the picture window.

To my delight, each time that I accompany Philip to Vermont, there is something different to look at and smell: lilacs in May, lupines in June, lady sleepers in July, phlox, goldenrod and hydrangeas in August until they dry up in the fall, when the tree colors are at their spectacular best. We often take a walk through the Bertocci woods. There is a long, shaded trail with ferns and wild berries near the ground and tall balsam and spruce among the elms and the maple trees. The soft maple leaves form a V and the hard maples a U, Philip tells me in his nature-lover mode. We try to clean the path as we walk, clearing the small branches and putting aside the bigger ones for firewood. The trail ends at a small pond, surrounded by cat-tails and wild flowers. It's too cold and slimy for us to swim in it, but it's perfect for ice-skating in the winter. The trail is also idyllic for cross country skiing in the long winter months, when the snow covers it as far as the eyes can see.

For Philip, a perfect summer day in Vermont is to go hiking to one of the nearby mountains. We often climb to the fire tower on Mount Elmore, where we eat a simple lunch of peanut butter sandwiches and apples, if Philip made it, or chorizo and cheese if I did. There is a stream that runs alongside the trail and you can hear the water trickling through the rocks and rushing in deeper parts. Four years ago, Philip said he loved me for the first time when we were atop of Mount Mansfield, on the flat rocks at the summit. It's a miracle I didn't choke on my sandwich, since I had already told him that I was crazy about him for months to no avail.

A perfect day for me is when I get to sit out back by the shed and write or read all afternoon. In the milk house I found some rickety blue chairs and an old farm table that I cover with a bright floral cloth, making a little impressionistic tableau. I love having our meals there, as if I were in some Monet painting. Sometimes I fall asleep on the old chaise lounge until I hear the wild turkeys come around the meadows, looking for the crab apples that have fallen from the nearby trees.

Not all is so idyllic in Wolcott. There are a few people who scare me if they stop by when I'm alone. There is Jim Lamoureux, a fellow who looks right out of *Deliverance*, Vermonter style: long, bushy hair, disheveled, face full of scars and all. He arrives in a beat-up old truck and quickly unloads his homemade all-terrain vehicle, which he uses for hunting. He was an old friend of Philip's father who gave him permission to hunt with a bow and arrow in their woods. He's very possessive about his rights and tries to evict anyone else he sees hunting there, particularly if they are using guns. He showed up one evening when I was alone to drop off some deer he had cleaned and frozen for us to take to Philadelphia for Thanksgiving. He worked his way into the porch and showed me pictures of the animals he had killed using his night vision goggles: wild turkeys, coyotes, deer. I pretended I was interested and that I wasn't afraid to become one of his tasty morsels, wondering how such a country bumpkin could know to work a digital camera so well at night, when I still struggle with mine in broad daylight.

Andy, the tree man, is another original character. He's been working with Philip for over twenty years, but has no intention of retiring; "I'd be a heap of trouble in a retirement home," he tells me. He dresses in old jeans, held up with suspenders and always wears huge galoshes to keep his legs dry when he walks in the fields. He carries a piece of cardboard, where he jots down how many of the Christmas trees he's going to cut each year. Philip marks with bright orange tape the ones he wants to keep for his own holidays and to barter with the neighbors.

There is a lot of bartering going on in Vermont. Philip lets the people who mow his pastures keep the hay as long as they maintain the fields cut. Firewood is exchanged for some goat cheese or fresh vegetables in the farm stand down the dirt road. I tell Philip how that is an old Italian tradition. I remember seeing it in a film as a young girl in Madrid, *Carousel Napolitano* with Sophia Loren: "tu mi dai una cosa a me, io ti do una cosa a ti" (you give something to me, I give something to you). Turns out that the Bertocci family comes originally from Naples and according to my theory, here they are continuing old world traditions in the new territories.

One evening we looked at his old family photographs and to me the Bertoccis, although born in this country, look much more like immigrants than my own family, particularly on his father's side, who came from Gaeta, outside Naples. Over the piano there is a big watercolor of the town harbor with the mountains in the background.

Old man Bertocci was also a college professor (another family trait we have in common). He taught French and comparative literature first at Bates and then Boston University. Philip is by far the darkest and the tallest of the four siblings. Two of them are blond and blue-eyed, like the mother, who was Finish. She looked beautiful in her Scandinavian way, but not as striking as my own mother with her killer Mediterranean looks. When the mother died, old grandfather Bertocci married Mary, a family friend, but she never was a bona fide member of the clan. Whenever something ugly shows up, an odd painting, an awkward screen in the porch, it's Mary's fault. The old Bertoccis retired to the farm house in Vermont and are buried in a country cemetery up the road.

I have a thousand questions, aside from the ones pertaining to the photos: do I want to take on another family's tastes, quirks, schedules and household? Never mind that I'm not allowed to touch anything in the house, particularly the old, smelly upholstered furniture and the torn-up homemade braided rug. I do get to cook tasty meals with Philip. He is a great everyday cook, not just a fancy one to impress guests as Peter was, but I tread lightly, I don't want to become the next Mary. He makes applesauce with two kinds of apples from the trees leftover from the time when there were orchards on their land. I make *panzanella* with fresh tomatoes, cucumbers and herbs.

Unfortunately, Philip's signature dish is *l'eau froide,* cold water. Take the time that, in the middle of a *paella* dinner with friends, Philip stated in no uncertain terms that he wasn't sure he wanted to retire or spend the rest of his life with me. Of course, my mother would say that I found the proverbial shoe, *el zapatito de tu pie,* something like if the shoe fits in English. She had a way of demystifying fairy tales. Didn't she know that if the shoe fit Cinderella, she was supposed to marry the prince?

An important question I also ask myself about my potential prince is "Could I take him to Spain?" I do the same thing with clothes, if I can't wear it in Madrid, I leave it in the store. Philip and I went to meet my family a couple of years ago and it went well, despite his lack of Spanish. We all know how much Europeans love to practice their English. The highlight of the trip was our visit to Extremadura, where I had never been, with the Rafael Moneo Roman Museum in Mérida being my very favorite. Philip loved the food: *cocido madrileño* (winter stew) at Lhardys and a *mariscada* (a shellfish orgy) at La Trainera. But his wow moment came when we were having a deconstructed Thanksgiving meal at my cousin's and he found himself surrounded by a Renoir sculpture, a Picasso ceramic plate and some Goya ink drawings. It pays to have some wealthy and cultivated relatives, I guess.

The trip to Ireland was our best journey together. I had signed up to go with a group during one of the times that Philip and I were not seeing each other and when he heard about it, he joined the group, too. At first we were going to have separate bedrooms, but we made up and decided to share the room and save money, and we didn't regret it. In preparation for our trip, we read all of Joyce in his postmodern glory. Well, neither one of us finished *Finnegan's Wake*. We took the Joyce walk through Dublin. Our guide, a graduate student from Trinity College, couldn't believe how well between the two of us we knew every detail of *Ulysses* and *Portrait of a Young Man*. I read Yeats for the first time and made my own mini festival of Irish films: *The Quiet Man, Michael Collins, The Dead, Ondine, Angela's Ashes.* That's something I love—making a research project out of every trip. I don't know if that makes me an old world nerd or is it part of my *chica moderna* profile.

It makes me sad to look at the few pictures of the two of us Philip allowed me to take on the cliffs of the Ring of Kerry and on the Giant's Causeway. We look happy together by the Calatrava Bridge over the river Liffey. What went wrong despite all our common tastes and shared experiences? Several of my friends tell me that I have the ideal relationship with Philip: we can count on each other, we can travel together, see each other when we want, but we don't have to put up with each other full time. Funny, how each of the people telling me that, happens to have a partner to snuggle up with in bed every night!

This summer, I'm again in Vermont with Philip. We have canoed in Wolcott Pond and watched the loons swimming alongside us; we have visited friends in the north tip of Lake Champlain, have seen an exhibit of Hopper watercolors in Middlebury College, have hiked the long trail up to Prospect Rock and have marveled at the views of the Lamoille River Valley along the way. All this is wonderful, but we ride mostly in silence, never talking about our feelings, there is no mention of the future, there is no first person plural to identify us. If Philip uses "we" he's talking about him and his siblings. I know that it takes two to tango and Philip and I only made it to the fox trot when we took dancing lessons.

I still find Vermont to be an enchanted place, but I'm sleeping alone in the downstairs bedroom while Philip sleeps upstairs in the old four poster bed. My pillows are on the middle of my bed, a sure sign, according to the new dating manuals, that I'm officially sleeping alone. There is no having the pillows on one side of the bed, as if I were waiting for prince charming to slip in and give me a wake-up kiss.

Flying Solo

Even though Peter was Jewish, he never expressed interest in visiting Israel. I, on the other hand, was always curious about the Middle East in general and the plight of the Jews in particular. I don't want to over intellectualize my feelings, but, as a Spaniard, I share an innate sense of guilt for the cruel historical past of my ancestors. I notice it when I travel in Latin America, when I encounter an old vestige of Sephardic culture, visiting the Jewish cemetery in Prague, for example, or something as simple as an ethnic recipe with its obvious old Spanish origin. I remember vividly the occasion a few years ago when I heard a song at a friend's Seder that sounded completely familiar. Without even thinking and despite being a terrible singer, I broke into song. I knew the words in Spanish to the very music that was being sung in Yiddish, so my feelings have, undoubtedly, a historical reason.

Thus, I was very excited when I found myself en route to Israel, one of my first trips flying solo. Actually, I wasn't all alone because Martha, a recent widow, was coming with me. Coincidentally, she lost her husband to the same illness that Peter suffered, esophageal cancer, and I tried to be a source of support for her while she went through a situation that was so eerily familiar to mine. Through it all, we had become friends and decided to travel together, even sharing a room, a tall order under any circumstances.

The day we arrived in Jerusalem, our first destination, there was a huge demonstration of Orthodox Jews. The whole city was closed and the traffic had completely grid-locked. The Ultra-Orthodox groups were asking for an extension of their deferment from military service.

The government had just voted to require them to serve as any other Israeli citizen, particularly because most of them don't hold jobs and rely heavily on government subsidies. Our Road Scholar bus had to drive for several hours around the periphery of the city until we reached the Prima Kings Hotel in the center of town. It was not an ideal way to start a trip, especially after a thirteen hour flight and a few more hours waiting for the rest of our fellow travelers at Ben Gurion Airport.

The hordes of demonstrators were dressed mostly in black; the men wearing the traditional fedora hats, with their long side curls, their prayer shawls around their shoulders and *tzitzit*, the long white strings hanging at their waists. The women were almost hidden under their wigs and scarves. There were many small children in strollers or walking about, looking like identical reproductions of their parents: the girls in dark colors and long printed dresses, the boys in the same Orthodox attire as their fathers. It was a moving sight because, despite the heavy police presence, there didn't seem to be any violence at all. Perhaps the apparent peace was due to the extreme safety measures. The stage was set for what would be the theme for the next two weeks: peace in the midst of chaos.

For me, one of the highlights in Jerusalem was our visit to the Wailing Wall. We have seen it so many times on the news that I thought I would recognize it immediately, but I was surprised to see that it's really a part of the Temple Mount, where now stands the largest and most important of the mosques in Jerusalem. The men and women were strictly separated by a partition. On the men's side the young boys were chanting, getting ready for Purim and on the women's side, the little girls were standing on chairs to peek at their counterparts, jealous, perhaps, of their merriment. As the well-prepared traveler that I like to be, I had a small notebook ready, from which I tore pages to share with our group. We wrote our own private prayers, folded them as tiny as possible and squeezed them into any crevice in the wall we could find. At first I wrote my usual prayers for my daughters and grandchildren, along with my thanks and wishes for a safe trip and stood back (no, I didn't ask for the elusive boyfriend). At the last minute, I decided to write one more note and ran back to the wall before my group would leave me behind. It was for Peter, telling him that I had forgiven him and that I wished him peace, wherever his spirit was now. I, for one, felt at peace. Suddenly, I found myself, appropriately, crying silently by the Wailing Wall.

Surprisingly, the lapsed Catholic in me surfaced and I felt remorse as we walked around the sites of the Holy Land: the Mount of Olives, the Via Dolorosa, the Church of the Holy Sepulcher, the Church of the Annunciation, the Garden of Gethsemane, Nazareth. I remember my Godmother Teresa, the only true believer on the Spanish side of the family, telling me about these holy places and how moved she was when she finally made the same trip with her church group from Valencia. Aunt Teresa passed away last fall and I've asked my cousins who is going to pray for us now; we better watch out or we are all going to end up in hell without this fervent intermediary.

We had several lectures on the Israeli-Palestinian conflict, but the diverse Catholics in the Holy Land don't get along either. We visited the Church of the Nativity in Bethlehem, off Manger Square, and found that the Greek Orthodox and the Armenians haven't been able to agree with their fellow Catholics on many issues, like the restoration of the church that, in the meantime, is falling down in neglect. Luckily, some of their holidays are observed on different days so they don't have to share the space all the time. Nevertheless, on the day we visited, there was a mix-up about which parts were open to the public and we almost weren't allowed to go inside the Grotto of the Nativity.

After three full days in Jerusalem, just when we were getting tired of going up and down the old cobblestone streets and fighting the tourist crowds, we left to tour the rest of the country on our comfortable bus. I loved this part of the trip: reading my travel books, taking notes, looking out the window, seeing the landscape change even faster than it does in Spain and on fast forward compared to the United States, where one can spend whole days on the highways without a change of scenery.

I wonder why I like to travel so much and realize that my father was redeeming himself from the grave. I learned to appreciate traveling from him when I was a little girl and I would go with him on his Vespa motor scooter to some towns close to Madrid: Toledo, Segovia, Avila, Salamanca. My father would lecture me with the most interesting details of each Roman ruin, medieval monastery or Gothic cathedral. We would eat in the most typical restaurants and venture off the main roads to find a significant spot, like the time he took me to the River Jarama to show me where an important battle of the Spanish Civil War was fought and many Republican soldiers like him had been killed by Franco's troops. My brother and I would take turns going with my father on short trips when we got good grades in school. My mother, lucky lady that she was, took trips all the way to Andalucía or the Pyrenees with him. It was never the same after we finally purchased our first car, a Fiat 600, and could travel together as a family.

The infrastructure throughout Israel is excellent; in fact, the roads are in better shape than in the United States. Jerusalem is built on a limestone mountain, thus most of its structures are constructed of this yellowish stone, with solar panels on the rooftops for heating and power supply. The land is fertile and completely cultivated despite its original desert dryness, thanks to a modern irrigation system. The olive groves reminded me of Southern Spain and the wheat fields could be anywhere in Castile.

On the first day on the road we visited Masada with its magnificent Roman ruins and a breathtaking view of the Dead Sea. We stopped at Qumran, home of the Dead Sea Scrolls and drove north through the fertile Jordan River Valley to Tiberias, on the Sea of Galilee. We stayed in one of the many kibbutzim that have been turned into lodging for tourism. Most of them were located in premium real estate and make for very comfortable accommodations, summer-camp-like with individual cottages and a common dining area. The Sea of Galilee has no waves, although in the afternoon, when the wind changes, there are sudden squalls. It's really a big lake, full of tilapia, perhaps a leftover from the biblical miracle.

Although there are a few kibbutzim left from their heyday in the sixties and seventies, the volunteer movement has for all effects ended. Degania, the kibbutz we visited, was one of the first founded in the 1920's, and it's typical of the few surviving ones in that they bring people to manage their finances and work their land (mostly Asians), while the members work outside in some nearby factory. Those who have stayed in the kibbutz and are still hanging on, can't really leave because they lack a retirement plan or social security.

Life on the road soon became routine. We were asked to take turns sitting in the front of the bus to give everyone a chance for a better view, but the two or three loud jokesters in the group preferred to sit in the back and laugh to their heart's content, so after a couple of days, we practically had assigned seats. Despite our differences we got along well. The eight single women in the group liked to sit near each other and close to our guide, Graeme Stone, while the couples cuddled together in the middle of the bus. I have to stop looking at the cozy couples and wondering what ever happened to me. Martha and I watched out for each other constantly, pointing out some quaint scene or hidden danger. There was an American born in Iran in the group who caused delays every time we had to show our passports. I was worried that I would also be flagged by the "Al" of my last name so I kept to myself the story of my family name, Alborch, "the tower" in Arabic, which my grandfather changed to the more Danish-sounding Alborg.

One of the women was actually traveling with the only single man of the group, although they had separate rooms. They met on another Road Scholar trip. For some reason, he was very attentive toward me and would comment daily on the outfit I had worn to dinner the evening before. Now, don't take me wrong, I would love to have a male travel companion, but I wasn't about to steal him in front of his lady friend. I spent the entire trip avoiding him and complementing her. Funny how he ended up front and center in so many of the pictures I took; there he is in the ruins in Amman and the Roman baths in Masada and next to me in the group picture we took in Petra.

There was a constant presence of armed guards patrolling the roads, particularly as we got closer to Jordan, and we had our own gun-toting policeman on the bus. The adventure turned into an ordeal when it came time to cross the border. We had to change buses and guides and go in and out of several security check points. For some unknown reason, my bag got held back along with that of a fellow traveler and the morning turned into afternoon, making us late for our first feast of Jordanian food.

We all loved the food in the Israeli hotels, despite the fact that, being Kosher, the breakfast buffet served only dairy and the evening menu had none at all. I have been trying to eat Israeli style since I got back from the trip: lots of fresh, raw vegetables for the first course and more vegetables cooked in unusual ways with very little meat— just enough for a kebab or a lamb stew—for the main course. Fresh and dried fruits with plenty of nuts for dessert, of course. If anything, the food in Jordan was even tastier because it was often made Lebanese style with more spices and exotic flavors. My favorite was the Meat Mansaf we ate at the Lebanese House in Jerash, where many famous people had eaten, even before we visited!

The weather was far from perfect for most of the trip. When we arrived in Israel, they were in the middle of a *sharav* weather pattern, which means that it was cloudy and cool, with strong winds blowing from the desert. It's like being in Los Angeles with the Santa Ana winds blowing. We could feel the sand grinding our teeth and our eyes were red and irritated. The same type of weather is called *khamasini* in Jordan, where, since the roads are in such deplorable condition, and the visibility was so poor, our bus ride on the Desert Highway was bumpy and scary, particularly, for those of us bookworms sitting in the front. When it started to rain the dust on the windshield turned to mud and it wasn't a pretty sight.

We arrived in Petra, Jordan, in the middle of a thunderstorm. At first we weren't sure if it was thunder or gunshots. I've never been so happy to be in the middle of an old-fashioned electrical storm! Although the official relations between Israelis and Jordanians are cordial, the political situation has had a negative impact on tourism, especially in Jordan. This turned out to be an advantage for us intrepid travelers, because we were upgraded to a luxury hotel, right outside the entrance to the ruins of Petra. I had heard of the marvels of this sight from several of my Spanish relatives and had anticipated this part of the trip like no other, but nothing prepared me for its majestic splendor. Despite the constant rain, our visit was memorable.

Some members of the group rode horses to enter through the Sikh Gorge while others rode in horse-drawn carriages through the canyon to the Treasury. There were also camel rides by the Monastery. I walked all the way in and out, appreciating everything I saw: the Roman walkways (very slippery with the rain), the burial caves, the spectacular rock formations, the immense ruins. It's hard to believe that this huge site was hidden for more than four centuries, abandoned by the Nabataeans, until 1812 when it was rediscovered by a Swiss traveler, Johan Ludwig Burckhardt.

In fact, it wasn't totally uninhabited, since the Bedouins lived in its caves, completely isolated from any civilization. The Bedouins have been relocated now to the adjoining valley and they are the only ones allowed to come in to Petra and peddle their wares. One of the most interesting stands was the one tended by Marguerite van Geldermalsen, a New Zealand-born nurse who married a Bedouin, learned Arabic, converted to Islam and lived in a 2000 year old cave with him and their three children. He died thirteen years ago and Marguerite has written her memoir, *Married to a Bedouin* (2006).

Now, how is that for an amazing story? She promptly signed a copy for me when she heard that I was a fellow widow and a writer as well.

Unlike our low-key guide in Israel, the Jordanian leader knew how to create suspense and drama on our trip. He showed up at breakfast the morning we were leaving for the Wadi Rum desert, warning us that all the rain had caused huge mudslides and the Desert Highway could be closed. It's true that there were rocks and mud in the middle of the road, but it didn't stop us as he warned. It turned out that all the rain had cleared the air and, although it was cold, the day in the desert was beautiful and sunny, without the sandy winds or the muddy rain. That doesn't mean that it lacked excitement. The Jeeps that we rode from the Seven Pillars of Wisdom in Wadi Rum were in a horrible state of disrepair. Furthermore, our young driver had to jump-start his vehicle by shorting two cables and drove one-handed as he texted on his iPhone. Lawrence of Arabia would have never tolerated such schizophrenia. It's one thing to be at the mercy of the weather and another to put our lives in the hands of a young Arabian punk.

Originally our trip was supposed to include Egypt, but due to the unstable political situation there, it was cancelled and more time in Jordan was added. I have to give credit to Road Scholar for good planning. Our two days of rest at a resort on the Dead Sea was just what we needed. For the first time, Martha and I asked to have our room changed to another with a better view. We had agreed in Amman, where our room had three small and uncomfortable beds that we would speak up next time. I remember laughing, thinking that perhaps three wives had stayed in that room, waiting for their sultan to come in to visit. We even thought we heard a knocking on the door that night, but good Christian ladies that we are, we didn't open it.

The Dead Sea, which is really a lake, less than fifty miles long and ten miles across, is the lowest point on earth, over 400 meters below sea level and thus—we were told—you can't get a sunburn there, since the UV rays don't reach you. At first, we didn't believe it any more than the fact that its mud has special therapeutic effects. I covered myself with my trusty 55 sunscreen and went around taking pictures of my mud-caked fellow travelers. But that evening, it was evident that no one was red from the sun, even those who hadn't used protection, although they didn't look ten years younger as the spa brochure promised either. I took advantage of the free time to catch up on my reading and journal writing. But I know I'm getting bored when I start shopping in the hotel boutique… time to get back on the road!

The cultural aspects of the trip were very rewarding. In each spot we had lectures by local scholars with lively discussions afterward. Road Scholar is true to its name on the brochure. The lecture while we were staying at the Dead Sea was particularly interesting. Father Hanna Kildani, Ph.D., a Catholic priest, spoke to us about Christianity and modern history in the Holy Land. He started by telling us that in Jordan there is freedom of worship, but not freedom of religion. He gave an example that Christians may marry among themselves, but not with Muslims. He also made it clear that not all Arabs are Muslims, there are Christian Arabs as well. Father Kildani works with Caritas, which is a Catholic institution that serves any religious denomination.

One of my favorite activities was the archeological dig we participated in our last day back in Israel, before the return trip to Philadelphia. The Temple Mount has an antiquity salvage operation in the Emek Tzurim Park in Jerusalem. We arrived in the midst of an awful downpour, completely wet and mud-covered, which meant that we fit right in with the young volunteers working there. Right away, we were divided into small groups and given buckets full of what looked like plain dirt. As soon as we spread its contents over a big sieve, we found hidden mosaics, glass, ceramic, metal and even bones. Every little bit was categorized and placed in separate containers with their proper labels. We couldn't keep any of the treasures we found, but we all got a certificate of participation. I could hear the rain pouring down on the tent and wondered if our flight would take off on time in the middle of this *sharav*, the same weather as we had the day we arrived.

It never fails; at the end of the trip people start complaining: too much time on the bus, the weather is horrible, their clothes are dirty and wet, not enough time to shop (the women) or too much time for shopping (the men)… It's true that traveling can be trying whether flying solo or with the best companion, as Martha was. But I don't complain; I realize that I haven't worried about a thing back home and I haven't even thought about my upcoming move to a smaller place and all I'll have to do when I get back. To me one of the best aspects of such a far-away trip is that it's all relative; flying to Europe now should be as easy as going to the West Coast or as easy as it was to go on a day excursion outside Madrid when I was a little girl.

Epilogue. No Corpses

I thought I had finished my memoir on widowhood just about the time I decided to sell my townhouse and downsize to a smaller condo in a high rise; down and up, so to speak. But as I went through the process, I realized that I hadn't completed my book after all. Selling the house is an important part of being a widow and it brought all kinds of memories and situations to the forefront again.

Peter and I moved into this gorgeous I. M. Pei townhouse in Philadelphia over thirteen years ago. We were barely able to afford it, but we bought it from friends who were eager to move away, and my family home in Madrid had just sold, giving me an unexpected small inheritance. At the time we were expecting to live there during our long retirements; two people working at home, one a musician, the other a writer, with over 3000 square feet to share. Peter's death interrupted all those plans and I found myself with one salary and one retirement plan in a place that was too big for only one person.

When I think about it, aside from the betrayal, not all the memories are rosy. There were already some red flags with this house from the very beginning. Unbeknownst to me, Peter had lost his job right before we moved in. It was a miracle that we qualified for a mortgage with just my professor's salary. Two years later he was diagnosed with cancer and from then on, the house was definitely my own responsibility, since, anyway, I was the one who really coveted the move to Center City Philadelphia from the suburbs. When Peter passed away, the market had changed for the worse. Furthermore, I was advised not to make any drastic changes in my lifestyle, so I stayed for several more years.

I don't know how I found the energy and the money to renovate the entire place during that time. I thought that my boyfriend Philip and I would share in this project, but he moved out in the middle of it, when the two main floors and the basement were still under construction. Maybe the remodeling was a factor in our breakup. After that, I kept the place in selling condition, waiting for the market to change. I even showed my home in the yearly Society Hill Open House Tour. I did enjoy its glamour, its high ceilings, the huge kitchen, the picture windows to the courtyard, the fireplaces, the shady city garden, the bidet in the master bathroom. I was not pleased with the high utility bills, the cold drafty windows, the leaky basement, the five flights of stairs, the crazy gardener next door.

As soon as the first news of a recovering real estate market started circulating, I put my house up for sale. There were at least two other recent widows in the courtyard and, with my usual haste, I didn't want to be the last one standing. The first people who looked at it bought it. When I was told that someone from Maine was coming with a cash offer, my daughters thought for sure it would be Stephen King! Who else could have that much cash on hand and insist in arriving on a Sunday evening? Just like that, it was sold and I cried when the wealthy couple from Maine, not the famous author, came over to sign the contract.

Small detail: a seller's market is not necessarily a buyer's heaven; who knew about the small time window in the fall before the real estate market shuts down for the holidays? Suddenly my home was sold and there were no two-bedroom condos for sale in the neighborhood I loved. I was sure I wanted to stay in the same area: same friends, gym and grocery store, same zip code and phone number. I ended up buying a friends' place I had seen the summer before and had dismissed with a quick: "lovely, but it's too small." Amazing what a real emergency will do for a hasty appraisal.

There were a million things to do, just four weeks before Christmas and two months before closing when I could become homeless. One advantage of downsizing is that there is more money for renovations. In all my prior moves, we had a very small budget left from the high mortgage to make any changes to the new abode. This time I, too, was paying cash and I planned to improve the condo to my heart's content. I had a main contractor, a kitchen designer, an electrician, painters, a closet planner, a plumber and a floor man to deal with. Thank goodness I am the queen of multitasking. I've never made so many lists in my life. It helped that I was the only one making the decisions and I didn't have to consult with anyone.

I ended up changing the floor in the bedrooms and all the doors, installing a built-in china cabinet, enlarging one bathroom and renovating the other, painting the entire place, adding a backsplash with American Arts and Crafts tiles in the kitchen and changing the floor in the terrace to a teak decking. I soon found out that the workmen were no different from college professors. They were very territorial, thoroughly proud of their work and quick to create a scene. No one got along with Mr. Torres, the floor man, and when he came all the other workers stayed away. The painters argued with the electrician, the plumber fought with the granite counter-top installer and the closet people made me sign a release when I brought in a stained-glass artist to make the china cabinet doors echo the chandelier. No wonder contractors don't have tenure; a unanimous decision would have been impossible, just like it was in my own Foreign Language Department.

I showed up one day in the middle of an argument between Vinnie, the painter, and Gordon, the electrician. I learned my lesson: make sure to call before coming to my own home. Later, a friend mentioned to me a memorable episode in *Murphy Brown*, the old sitcom, with a prima donna painter. I watched it on YouTube and thought it was hysterical. The following day I made the mistake of mentioning it to Vinnie, thinking I was being funny and trying to break the ice from the bad karma of the day before. Big mistake; Vinnie went into a tantrum, saying that I, of all people, with my Spanish accent, would be aware of stereotypes, and how sick and tired he was of hearing about the *Murphy Brown* episode. I quickly told him that he was the best painter I had ever had, which happens to be the truth, and we were best friends from then on.

Every day there was some new drama. The bathroom vanity somehow didn't get ordered on time and I had to go to a supply store in South Philly to choose another one in stock. Angelo, a sexy Italian with a pony tail, called me "honey" and "dear" and held on to my arm through his entire line of bathroom fixtures. The feminist in me didn't know whether to laugh or reprimand him when he planted a juicy kiss on my cheek as I left. I think I blushed.

Most days I had fun going through my belongings, deciding what to keep, what to throw away or what to give my children. The furniture part was easy; my two grown daughters kept most everything and, since they live close by, I get to see my old furnishings along with my grandchildren when I visit. A lot of the books went to academic friends, the Saint Joseph's University library and the thrift shop. I hate to admit it, but getting rid of my clothes, shoes and dishes was the hardest part. The closer I got to the moving date, the more anxious I became. Finally, I decided to join an American lifestyle tradition by taking a small storage space.

I had never been to a storage facility. This one is on a pier on the Delaware River. It's huge and cold, even the heated units, like the one I rented. I had no idea how elaborate the rental process is. I had to sign a contract and agree to all the rules of the lease. I couldn't believe my ears when the attendant told me that "there are no corpses allowed." "Excuse me?" I said feeling and looking thoroughly confused. Obviously, some people have used their storage units for criminal purposes. No wonder I am afraid to go to my unit by myself, which is all the way in the back of the building.

While I was purging my house, I was getting rid of all of Peter's possessions; the last vestiges of the shipwreck. I gave all of his mother's paintings to the Segal siblings. Well, I kept the one with the woman by a blue vase, which now hangs in my bedroom. I even returned all the files that Lisa, my sister-in-law, had given me about her father. I wouldn't be writing about that side of the family anymore. On my last trip to Spain I found letters written by my parents during the Spanish Civil War, and that is the extent of family memoirs I want to tackle. Hopefully that will be my next project, although it means that I have to go back to writing in Spanish. It's interesting how to change my language is similar to changing my life.

In some ways, I feel guilty for breaking the "No corpses" rule, because the last of Peter's belongings have ended up in the storage unit. All his guitars have been sold, with the exception of the Romantic and the Baroque ones, which are still on consignment at the Guitar Salon in San Francisco. My nephew took his books because he is also a musician and he was so fond of Peter. His sheet music collection went to the Music School at Temple University in his memory. Ironically, I put some leftover documents: death certificates, will, old passports, diplomas, music awards, some correspondence and photographs in a Black Label wine box. How sad that Peter's remains ended up in one of the simple boxes from the liquor store I used for my move. Such an exuberant man, who lived life to the fullest, who loved more than I knew, who was so loved by so many—including me—was now reduced to a box in a storage unit.

The closing day for my new condo coincided with the building's Christmas party and at the last minute, although I still hadn't moved there, I decide to attend. It was held in the rooftop solarium, which opens to the pool area in the summer. It may be a livelier place then, but in the middle of the snowy winter, it seemed a little stale and dark. There were some tables with simple refreshments, one with wine and punch in the corner, and others with candles and Christmas tablecloths. I knew very few people, just a couple of ladies from my gym. What I noticed right away was how many ugly sweaters—including my own—were present and how many people there had walkers and even wheelchairs. At that moment, I felt as if I were moving into a retirement community, and I wasn't ready for that yet. I left the party feeling depressed.

The strangest part was that the next afternoon when I arrived to check on my contractors, several of the women I had seen at the party were at the front desk instead of the regular, uniformed doormen. At first I thought I was having a stroke and seeing visions. How could that be? When the women greeted me by name, "Welcome, Concha, it was so nice meeting you last evening," I started to think it was all a dream or perhaps a nightmare. Then I remembered one of the ladies' names, Elaine, and I asked her what was going on. Why were they working in the lobby? Turned out that they were volunteering—they do it every year so all the doormen can have their own Christmas party together. In walkers or wheelchairs, these sweet women are part of the community, and I've found out since then that they congregate at the condo parties because they don't get to go out as much as they would want to. Lesson learned, Concha.

Something that has definitely helped me with the transition to a smaller place and condo living is that I grew up in a similar setting in Madrid. I didn't realize it until I moved in and I could hear the screaming voices of the children across the hall, running to the elevator. When we were children we weren't allowed to ride the elevator down and could come up only if we were accompanied by an adult. Of course, the building had a mere seven floors and not thirty-one like this condo. My apartment in Madrid had a hairdresser and a deli downstairs like this one, but it didn't remind me of a retirement home. We also could smell the food cooking in the hallway. I remember that my father, with his accustomed bad mood, would come in and announce that the neighbors were having brussel sprouts again. "As if we didn't know already," my mother would respond, rolling her eyes. They say that smells are our most durable memories and I think it's true, because I feel at home when my Greek neighbors are cooking spanakopita; it reminds me of my mother's tasty meals.

I had the walls of my apartment painted in an earthy palette of terracotta and greens like the ones I saw in the Tuscany countryside last summer. The living/dining area and my study face south and are full of light and brightness, even on rainy days. My bedroom is in a western corner and I can see the sunset and the exciting city view of the Philadelphia skyscrapers and Washington Square. The kitchen is open to the living room, creating an illusion of space. Despite many suggestions from well-meaning friends, who assured me that small furniture is best in a small apartment, I brought with me a few large pieces like my two leather sofas and the wicker chairs. I did buy a smaller bed, a rod-iron queen size, very appropriate, since the king never showed up or, more likely, disappeared from my life. I exchanged the huge Indian Mahindra rug from Material Culture for a similar one in deep reds of the same vintage. No wonder I love this place; I'm surrounded by some of my favorite things!

An important step in my transition was to get rid of all the old TVs and the convoluted music system that were left over from the Peter Segal era. After he died, no one could make the VCR work or figure out the five speakers he installed in his studio. In this apartment I have a smart HD TV, a CD unit that even plays Spanish films and a Bose sound bar that makes any speaker obsolete. To go with my new *"chica moderna"* profile I can stream the radio anywhere with my tablet, show my picture files through the TV and load as many apps as I want. Never mind that I still prefer making real paper albums of my special trips.

One of the reasons I feel so much at home in this new place is because it has a small terrace. Again, I'm reminded of my family's flat in Madrid, with its two large balconies, where I used to play with Manolita, my neighbor, and read during naptime when I got older. Here I can see as far as the Walt Whitman Bridge, the ships anchored in the Delaware River and the Platt Bridge next to the Philadelphia Airport. In the afternoons, in the distance, the planes glide for their landing one after the other in steady succession. On the snowy days we had when I first moved in, I felt like I was in a Christmas snow globe. During a storm the view can disappear like the changing backdrop in a theater and I can only see the Colonial townhouses down below. Now I have planted herbs, some pansies and some evergreens, which I hope will thrive in the spring sunshine.

The very best part of my new apartment is, without a doubt, the location. It's situated in one of the most beautiful parks in the city. Philadelphia was built around four strategic squares in a very European scale. Washington Square, where I live, is the closest to the historical area; Independence Hall, the Liberty Bell and the Constitution Center are close neighbors. The Athenaeum and several old buildings from when the city was a publishing Mecca have been turned into luxury condos surrounding the square. It isn't the Retiro Park or even Central Park, but on warm days there are plenty of dog walkers, runners, and people picnicking on the grass. Next to the Memorial Monument there is a big fountain, where children play on hot summer days, despite the signs warning not to let children and dogs into the water.

I have already started entertaining in my new digs. I prefer to have small dinner groups instead of large parties but, since my family has grown, we can easily be ten around the table or even more. Last week I opened the French farm table to its full length and we could all fit around it, a miracle really. I had to use the chairs from the terrace to accommodate everyone. It was a pseudo Easter dinner with little baskets full of jelly beans as nametags. For the first time the grandchildren ate on good china dishes –the Melamine plates got tossed away in the move. They looked so grown up, even though they asked to be excused as soon as they finished the rolls.

The grandchildren love to come into the city. This time they arrived with their parents on the suburban train, no parking worries that way. After dinner we rode the elevator to the rooftop to see the city lights at night. "My ears popped," screamed one after the other on the way up and then commented how they had vertigo, looking at the view from the solarium. They quickly took pictures with their iPhones and sent them to friends. The city glistened as far as the eyes could see, over the stadiums on the south side and all the way to the neon colors of Liberty One and the Comcast Center skyscrapers to the West. William Penn looked dwarfed and obscured on top of City Hall by the brighter, newer lights. My three grandchildren happen to have summer birthdays and they want to have a pool party to celebrate them this summer. They think it's cool to have a grandmother who lives in a high-rise. They don't know a thing about downsizing.

The weirdest thing is that I feel different since I moved. I am less of a widow here and more of a single woman. I guess my divorce from Peter is final now. There are no memories attached to this place of any man in my life. There is no room either to accommodate a partner dead or alive; I have filled up every closet to the rim, and then some (remember the storage unit). In theory my study could double as a guestroom; there is a trundle bed that opens up when the children spend the night with me. But I don't think that a grownup would fit comfortably there. I have more than a room of my own; I have an apartment of my own. Philip has mentioned that he would like to stay overnight sometime, our password for getting the benefits he's earned. And I say, "Soon, but not yet. I'm still getting my bearings."

Today a reporter from *The Philadelphia Inquirer* came over to interview me for an article in the Real Estate Section that appears on Sundays. They want to feature my downsizing expertise now that so many people—widows in particular—want to move to a smaller place in the city. I was a little hesitant in agreeing to do it. It would be very ironic if I became a celebrity due to my decorating skills instead of my writing. I'll have to make sure they mention that I'm indeed a writer and that I have a book, a memoir about the troubles and tribulations of being a modern widow ready to be published. This could be all the publicity I can get.

About the Author

Concha Alborg was born in Spain during the difficult years after the Spanish Civil War and went to school in Madrid until she emigrated with her parents to the United States, where she finished high school. More than any other event in her life, this move defines who she is, an immigrant living between two cultures. She may seem Americanized to her Spanish relatives, but she is from another country as far as her daughters are concerned. Although Concha fits well enough in both cultures, a tell-tale Spanish accent marks her speech as well as her writing.

Concha Alborg earned an MA from Emory University and a PhD in Spanish Literature from Temple University. In addition to numerous academic publications on contemporary women writers, she has been actively writing fiction and creative non-fiction. Recently, she left Saint Joseph's University, where she was a professor for over twenty years, to write full time. She has published two collections of short stories: *Una noche en casa* (Madrid, 1995) and *Beyond Jet-Lag* (New Jersey, 2000) and a novel, *American in Translation: A Novel in Three Novellas* (Indiana, 2011).

Concha Alborg didn't think that anything could hurt her more than the death of her husband from cancer, but hours after his death she learned how wrong she was. Within days of being made a widow, she discovered that her marriage and her husband were not what she had envisioned. In *Divorce After Death. A Widow's Memoir*, with a unique point of view, due to her bi-cultural background, and a self-deprecating humor, she takes us on a personal journey. Her strength and determination to build a new life led her down a path that allowed her to reject the veil of widowhood and instead embrace a life of happiness, love and acceptance.

Concha Alborg lives and writes in Philadelphia. See more information about the author at www.conchaalborg.com

Reviews

Concha Alborg took over where Oscar Wilde left out. If the portraitist of Dorian Gray stated, in unmistakable terms, that nature imitates art, Alborg´s ***Divorce after Death. A Widow´s Memoir*** transformed life, and also death, into live literature. From a narrative perspective this is nothing short of a prodigy.

Peter Segal, a guitarist and untenured professor of Music, was married to Concha for over twenty years, and he died from esophageal cancer after enduring surgery, chemotherapy, and even a tour of boreal Sweden in the closing years of his life. He withstood his fate without a single lament or protest.

Almost immediately, after her husband´s demise, Concha found out that throughout the twenty years of their marriage the guitarist maintained carnal and epistolary amorous relations with a seraglio of other women, apparently before and after ageing and cancer made him impotent.

The widow´s irate reaction was as quick as lightning. She "divorced" her spouse, and started taking long trips and short lasting lovers. Nevertheless she could not avoid, much less delete, her memories of Peter. Almost at the end of her pilgrimage, she found herself in Jerusalem, crying by the Wailing Wall, and leaving in one of its cracks a carefully folded message for Peter that I believe must have been the very first draft of this *Divorce After Death,* a real masterpiece in the so-called coming up genre of autobiographical non-fiction.

Oscar Wilde would have been delighted to see how his proverbial dictum proved to be true, and life becomes the tentative, mimicking sketch of future literature.

--Carlos Rojas, Charles Howard Candler Professor of Spanish, Emeritus, Emory University

Concha Alborg mediates her widowhood through an insightful memoir where lived moments and art mix in the crucible of a betrayed-but-not-defeated woman aware of her power to heal her wounds as a victor, not a victim.

Divorce after Death is a memorable memoir of "transit": sometimes painful, sometimes joyful, and always honest. The last chapters left me awestruck for their artistry.

--Adriana Lewis Galanes, Professor Emerita, Temple University

In **Concha Alborg's** book, *Divorce after Death. A Widow's Memoir,* her personality and grace emerge with a well-defined profile of an intellectual, a feminist and a postmodern woman. She is as well a sensitive, strong mother, a wife and grandmother. The content of the intertwining vignettes offer a diversity of situations and anecdotes around the elusive theme of happiness. As Antonio Machado said: "Happiness passed through your home, but it doesn't visit twice." Concha Alborg in her book is there to contradict the Spanish poet. She throws herself into life intensely, creating her own magic. When she places her feet on the sand and sees her image on a seashell, she reaffirms her own way, made by herself.

In her book, Concha Alborg's travels transform life into an adventure, which is what really matters, and she describes them with an experienced and keen eye. Her impressions on Bolivia, for example, probe into the depths of a Spaniard on a Latin American land. She travels through half the world or a world and a half to get to know, to investigate, to learn. She is not passing by anywhere. She is living the experience and her readers live it with her, they go to the heights with her and fly low when she does. Her tears at the Wailing Wall become a climax, purifying and liberating her. She has arrived at the pinnacle of the great souls who are in a state of grace because they can forgive. She calls it "the highlight of her visit," but it's more than that. It is a way to find peace, for a time at least.

In *Divorce after Death*, there are encounters and misunderstandings. Her readers laugh with her, not at her. Like the guy who thinks that she is on vacation when she travels abroad with her students, showing the lack of understanding of her profession, as she wisely tells us.

What a pleasure to go into Concha's kitchen, smelling her sauces and condiments, feeling the aromas of a fortifying wine that goes into our bones. The recipes that she generously includes have gone through the cultural sieve and they are authentically Spanish, but accessible to the American table. She tells us of her origins, her parents, her exodus, her family. Everything is relevant.

The reader feels like he or she is going with Concha to the opera, to concerts, on walks, to museums, to wineries, to the beach and on her dates. One can see her writing in a cozy corner, traversing Italy with Peter or in the fancy cruise with death stalking him while she is loving him and taking care of him. His death is synthesized in his pale hands, loved and lost hands that hold her pain. She becomes a widow, but prefers to take care of herself and to be called single. The letter that titles the book, is a diatribe full of irony, sarcasm, anger and profound disenchantment. It is a master piece in its genre, superior to *Cinco horas con Mario* by Miguel Delibes and other diatribes.

All the aspects of Concha Alborg's memoir demonstrate the impact and quality of her writing. The titles, the structure of each chapter and the book as a whole are coherent and give a meaning to life itself. The journey, apparently exterior, turns out to be an interior journey of encounter with herself. Although she may feel that she is adrift sometimes, like going through life on roller-skates, everything adds up, everything helps to shape her. The language and the narrative techniques, the dramatic and poetic elements give variety to the text and cause an emotional impact on the readers. This is a heartwarming and heartbreaking story. This is a fully lived life turned into literature. This is a sincere book, diverse and moving, written by an authentic writer.

--Cecilia Castro Lee, Professor Emerita, University of West Georgia

Poet Mary Oliver refers to "the dark heart of the story/that is all the reason for its telling". In her memoir **Concha Alborg** goes straight there, to the dark heart of the story: accidentally discovering right after her husband's passing that he had been a serial cheater throughout their marriage.

Recovering from the death of a beloved spouse after caring for him through a harrowing three-year battle with esophageal cancer is difficult enough without such an added factor. One might expect that Alborg's memoir would be bitter and brimming with resentment. The startling fact is that it is not. Showing an admirably strong sense of self, she refuses to become a victim. True, eight years have passed, a distance perhaps sufficient to soothe the soul and heal the wounds. But that alone does not account for the measured tone, a tone that does not preclude heartrending moments of sadness as well as humorous episodes. Alborg's spunk and her talent for delighting in life–even at its most absurd or challenging–trump the betrayal.

Someone has said that the best way to set the world straight is to give to others what you need to get. And here it is in all its glory, the painful truth exposed and shattering Peter's reputation as the family's stalwart nice guy. The stark contrast between the husband's veil of lies and the wife's unblinking candor in presenting the events is deeply moving.

So many questions remain. Alborg wonders how she did not know, never suspected anything amiss. The reader ponders why the husband did not erase his hard drive when he went home for hospice care. Someone (possibly a male!) might ask whether Peter was not entitled to a private geography since Concha never hurt or lacked for anything during their long relationship. Or to what extent indeed did the discovery help Alborg get over her husband's death? All these imponderables merit reflection and provide fertile ground for discussion. In other words, *Divorce after Death: A Widow's Memoir* is a perfect read for book clubs that are willing to explore the thorny and ever fascinating terrain of infidelity. And it would be the ultimate poetic justice if the betrayal were to turn out to be the basis for a best-selling book!

--Cristina de la Torre, Emerita, Emory University

Divorce after Death. A Widow's Memoir is a moving book; it's entertaining, diverse and at the same time it has characteristics of a sociological essay. **Concha Alborg** captures how American people talk, their mannerisms and costumes. In my opinion, this is Alborg's most American book.

I want to point out how well Concha Alborg writes, the finesse in which she describes the places and people and how the reader can see the different types, telling us their most significant traits, both the amusing or ridiculous. It is all full of vitality. At the same time I am in awe of her extraordinary candid quality, how she opens her life to the reader with absolute innocence.

I especially liked the variety and richness of *Divorce after Death,* which gives it it's a quality of its own. It's very interesting to point out two aspects that overlap in this book. On one side, there is the widowhood story and her subsequent discovery of the betrayal and the pain it caused. On the other hand, the author has an ironic point of view, full of humor, about all the events that surround the life of a widow: the loneliness of a different life and the possibility of other relationships.

The ending of the book, with the move to a new apartment is most suggestive; a new life in a smaller place, full of light, in the center of town of a great city. The reader feels like going there to see the author, to find her anew in that life that she is constructing for herself.

--Inés Alberdi, Catedrática, Universidad Complutense

I found **Concha Alborg's** memoir truly enthralling—the story of a widow who ends up divorcing her late husband. Although the warning at the beginning of the book—the "spoiler alert"—may seem ill-advised at first, it works surprisingly well as a strategy that captivates the reader. In the role of a voyeur to someone else's life, I could not stop reading to find out what could have happened to a happily married woman to divorce her husband after his death. As I finished the book, I felt a tremendous admiration for an enterprising and resourceful widow who makes her own life, a life full of accomplishments in spite of the obstacles she encounters. This is an uplifting story, full of hope and emotion. It is also an immigrant's story, the story of a woman who juggles between two cultures, two sets of values and expectations.

--María-Inés Lagos, Spanish Professor, University of Virginia

Made in the USA
Middletown, DE
10 June 2019